Early Speculative Bubbles and Increases in the Supply of Money

Early Speculative Bubbles and Increases in the Supply of Money

Douglas E. French

Second Edition

*To Deanna,
for loving me through
the boom and the bust.*

First edition ©1992 by Douglas E. French
Second edition © 2009 by the Ludwig von Mises Institute and published under the Creative Commons Attribution License 3.0. http://creativecommons.org/licenses/by/3.0/

Ludwig von Mises Institute
518 West Magnolia Avenue
Auburn, Alabama 36832
www.mises.org

ISBN: 978-1-933550-44-2

Table of Contents

Introduction vii

Chapter 1—The Greater Fool Theory.   1

Chapter 2—Tulipmania 11

Chapter 3—Free Coinage, the Bank of Amsterdam,
and Tulipmania 19

Chapter 4—John Law, Genius or Swindler. 35

Chapter 5—John Law's Monetary Theories. 41

Chapter 6—The Mississippi Bubble 51

Chapter 7—The South Sea Bubble. 75

Chapter 8—Increases in the Supply of Money, Speculative
Bubbles, and the Austrian Malinvestment Theory 105

Bibliography. 119

Index 127

Introduction

As all the world economies writhe in financial pain from the cleansing of the largest bubble in financial history, the question is being asked—how could this happen? Of course the usual answers are trotted out—human greed, animal spirits, criminal fraud, or capitalism itself. Modern financial history has been a series of booms and busts that seem to blend together making one almost indistinguishable from the next. The booms seduce even the most conservative into taking what in retrospect appear to be outlandish risks speculating on investment vehicles they know nothing about.

In response to the financial meltdown, central banks are slashing interest rates to nearly zero and growing their balance sheets exponentially. With no more room to lower rates, central bankers now speak of a "quantitative easing" policy which in plain English means "creating money out of nowhere." But no one is shocked or horrified by this government counterfeiting. All this, after the U.S. central bank—the Federal Reserve—has already, at this writing, increased the M-2 money supply 11-fold ($686 billion to $8.2 trillion) since August of 1971 when the U.S. dollar's last faint ties to gold were severed.

While history clearly shows that it is this very government meddling in monetary affairs that leads to financial market booms and the inevitable busts that follow, mainstream economists either deny that financial bubbles can occur or claim that the "animal spirits" of market participants are to blame. Economists running central banks even claim that it is impossible to identify asset bubbles. Meanwhile, the Austrian School stands alone in pointing the finger at government intervention in monetary affairs as the culprit.

Austrian economists Ludwig von Mises and Friedrich A. Hayek's Austrian business cycle theory provides the framework to *explain* speculative bubbles. The Austrian theory points out that it is government's increasing the supply of money that serves to lower interest rates below the natural rate or the rate that would be set by the collective time preferences of savers in the market. Entrepreneurs react to these lower interest rates by investing in "higher order" goods (e.g., factories and machinery) in the production chain, as opposed to consumer goods.

Despite these actions by government, consumer time preferences remain the same. There is no real increase in the demand for higher order goods and instead of capital flowing into what the unfettered market would dictate—it flows into malinvestment. The greater the monetary expansion, in terms of both time and enormity, the longer the boom will be sustained.

But eventually there must be a recession or depression to liquidate not only inefficient and unprofitable businesses, but malinvestments in speculation—whether it is stocks, bonds, real estate, art, or tulip bulbs.

This book was my master's thesis (with just a couple of slight changes and additions) written under the direction of Murray Rothbard and it examines three of the most famous boom and bust episodes in history. Government monetary intervention, although different in each case, engendered each: Tulipmania, the Mississippi Bubble, and the South Sea Bubble.

As the seventeenth century began, the Dutch were the driving force behind European commerce. Amsterdam was the center of this trade and it was in this vibrant economic atmosphere that tulipmania began in 1634 and climaxed in February 1637. At the height of tulipmania, single tulip bulbs were bid to extraordinary amounts with the Witte Croonen tulip bulb rising in price 26 times in a month's duration. But when the market crashed: "Substantial merchants were reduced almost to beggary," wrote Charles Mackay, "and many a representative of a noble line saw the fortunes of his house ruined beyond redemption."[1]

In 1716, the French government was on the verge of bankruptcy and its citizens were fed up with their government's currency depreciation, recoinage schemes and increased tax collections. The situation was ripe for the notorious John Law's monetary magic which was to "lighten the burden of the King and the State in lowering the rate of interest" on France's war debts and to increase the supply of money to stimulate the French economy. Ultimately, the scheme, which was the Mississippi Company, unraveled and an outraged French public ultimately forced the Regent to place the once revered Law under house arrest.

While John Law was struggling to keep his Mississippi bubble inflated, across the English Channel, a nearly bankrupt British government looked on with envy, believing that Law was working a financial miracle. Sir John Blunt followed Law's example with his South Sea Company, which in exchange for being granted monopoly rights to trade with South America, agreed to refinance that government's debt.

The company had no real assets, but that didn't matter as speculators bid the share price higher and higher, spawning the creation of dozens of other "bubble companies." The South Sea Company lobbied the British government to pass a Bubble Act that would shut down these new companies that were competing for investor capital. Ironically, it was the enforcement of that act that burst the bubble with South Sea Company shares falling nearly 90 percent in price.

Although these episodes occurred centuries ago, readers will find the events eerily similar to today's bubbles and busts: low interest rates, easy credit terms, widespread public participation, bankrupt governments, price inflation, frantic attempts by government

---

[1]Charles Mackay, *Extraordinary Popular Delusions and the Madness of Crowds* (London: Richard Bentley, New Burlington Street), p. 95.

to keep the booms going, and government bailouts of companies after the crash.

Although we don't know what the next asset bubble will be, we can only be certain that the incessant creation of fiat money by government central banks will serve to engender more speculative booms to lure investors into financial ruin.

The Greater Fool Theory 1

Speculative bubbles have occurred throughout history. These episodes are characterized by a continuous sharp rise in the price of a particular asset or group of related assets, leading to further price increases driven by new speculators seeking profits through even higher prices. These higher prices are driven by the potential profits to be made through trading, rather than the earning capacity or economic value of the asset. These speculative manias then come to abrupt and dramatic endings, as expectations change and buyers quickly become sellers, in mass. The consequences are often disastrous, with the ensuing crash inflicting financial pain on the region or country involved. Euphoria turns to despair as the mandatory readjustment that takes place in the economy creates massive worker dislocation and great numbers of bankruptcies.

Contemporary economists' views concerning speculative bubbles vary. The Rational Expectations School questions whether speculative bubbles can happen at all, given rational markets. Charles Kindleberger concisely gives the rational expectations viewpoint:

> Rational expectations theory holds that prices are formed within the limits of available information by market participants using standard economic models appropriate to the circumstances. As such, it is claimed, market prices cannot diverge from fundamental values unless the information proves to have been widely wrong. The theoretical literature

uses the assumption of the market having one mind and one purpose.[1]

History tells a different story, of course. Market speculators at various times in history have bid up prices to extraordinary levels, not based upon fundamental values, but with the expectation of selling the asset in question at an even higher price and thus making a profit. This is sometimes referred to as the "greater fool theory."

John Maynard Keynes spends the whole of chapter 12 of *The General Theory of Employment, Interest, and Money* discussing speculation and bubbles, pointing to five factors which foster these episodes: (1) neophyte investors owning an increased proportion of capital investment; (2) the day-to-day price fluctuations having an excessive influence over the market; (3) violent changes in the mass psychology of ignorant individuals changing asset valuations; (4) professional investors devoting their skills to "anticipating what average opinion expects the average opinion to be;" and (5) confidence, or lack of, in the credit markets.[2]

Keynes metaphorically describes speculative markets:

> Nor is it necessary that anyone should keep his simple faith in the conventional basis of valuation having any genuine long-term validity. For it is, so to speak, a game of *Snap*, of Old Maid, of Musical Chairs—a pastime in which he is victor who says *Snap* neither too soon nor too late, who passes the Old Maid to his neighbor before the game is over, who secures a chair for himself when the music stops.[3]

---

[1] Charles P. Kindleberger, "Bubbles," in *The New Palgrave: A Dictionary of Economics*, John Eatwell, Murray Milgate, and Peter Newman, eds., 4 vols. (New York: The Stockton Press, 1987), p. 281.

[2] John Maynard Keynes, *The General Theory of Employment, Interest, and Money* (New York: Harcourt, Brace & World, 1964), pp. 153–58.

[3] Ibid., pp. 155–56.

Keynes also touches upon the consequences of speculative bubbles and manias:

> Speculators may do no harm as bubbles on a steady stream of enterprise. But the position is serious when enterprise becomes the bubble on a whirlpool of speculation. When the capital development of a country becomes a by-product of the activities of a casino, the job is likely to be ill-done.[4]

Ironically, it is due to a Keynesian economic policy and its monetary apparatus, i.e., that of expanding the supply of money to increase economic activity, that speculative price bubbles and manias are engendered. This was exemplified by John Law, whose system (driven by a huge increase in the supply of money) created the Mississippi Bubble in France. Law, who preceded Keynes by two hundred years, held many of the same views as Keynes. As Charles Rist explains:

> It is said that history repeats itself. One can say the same thing about economists. At the present time there is a writer whose ideas have been repeated since Keynes, without ever being cited by name. He is called John Law. I would be curious to know how many, among the Anglo-Saxon authors who have found again, all by themselves, his principal arguments, have taken the trouble to read him.[5]

However, there are economists who do not feel the episode in early eighteenth century France was a bubble. As Peter Garber writes:

> That Law's promised expansion never materialized does not imply that a bubble occurred in the modern sense of the word. After all, this was not the last time that a convincing economic idea would fracture in practice. One respectable group of modern economists or another have described Keynesian economics, supply side economics, monetarism, fixed exchange

---

[4]Ibid., p. 159.

[5]Quoted in Joseph T. Salerno,"Two Traditions in Modern Monetary Theory: John Law And A.R.J. Turgot," *Journal des Economistes et des Etudes Humaines* 2 (June/September 1991): 368–70.

rate regimes, floating exchange rate regimes, and the belief in rational expectations in asset markets as disastrously flawed policy schemes. Indeed, elements of the first three were primary components in Law's scheme.[6]

Other contemporary economists pursue the explanation of speculative bubbles through mathematical formulas. It is not surprising that this search for empirical evidence has produced nothing that aids in our understanding of these episodes. The tools of econometrics were designed to explain the movement of lifeless particles, not the activities of humans, who act with purpose to improve their condition in life. In an article by Robert Flood and Robert Hodrick, it is pointed out that "academic economists conducted relatively little formal empirical analysis of actual markets until recently, probably because economist's analytical and statistical tools were inadequate."[7] Messrs. Flood and Hodrick go on to pursue the case that "the widespread adoption of the rational expectations hypothesis provided the required underpinning for theoretical and empirical study of the issues."[8] But, as was pointed out above, those in the Rational Expectations School, through their belief that all market participants can foretell the future, and thus only act rationally, virtually rule out the potential for speculative bubbles. Unsurprisingly, after surveying the current empirical literature concerning bubbles, they come to the conclusion that "the current empirical tests for bubbles do not successfully establish the case that bubbles exist in asset prices."[9]

This present volume contends, based upon historical experience, that speculative bubbles do occur and that these bubbles are precipitated by a large increase in the supply of money. This monetary

---

[6]Peter Garber, "Famous First Bubbles," *Journal of Economic Perspectives* 4 (Spring 1990): 46–47.

[7]Robert Flood and Robert Hodrick, "On Testing for Speculative Bubbles," *Journal of Economic Perspectives* 4 (Spring 1990): 85.

[8]Ibid., p. 86.

[9]Ibid., p. 99.

intervention creates situations that manifest themselves in malinvestment, i.e., speculative bubbles. What then follows is the required period of readjustment, i.e., crash and depression. This sequence of events is similar to the Minsky/Kindleberger sequence of events that characterize stock market booms and busts, as outlined by Antoin Murphy:

1. The market rise starts off because of some *exogenous shock* such as war, the end of a war, a technological or natural resource discovery, or "a debt conversion that precipitously lowers interest rates." The shock creates new opportunities for profit, and a boom is engendered.

2. The boom is nurtured by an expansion of bank credit which expands the money supply. Alternatively, the velocity of circulation increases.

3. As increased demand pushes up the prices of goods and financial assets, new profit opportunities are found and confidence grows in the economy. Multiplier and accelerator effects interact and the economy enters into a *"boom or euphoric state."* At this point *overtrading* may take place.

4. Overtrading may involve:

    a. Pure speculation, that is over-emphasis on the acquisition of assets for capital gain rather than income return;

    b. Overestimation of prospective returns by companies;

    c. Excessive gearing involving the imposition of low cash requirements on the acquisition of financial assets through buying on margin, by installment purchases, and so on.

5. When the neophytes, attracted by the prospect of large capital gains for a small outlay, become numerous in the market, the activity assumes a separate abnormal momentum of its own. Insiders recognize the danger signals and move out of securities into money.

6. A *financial distress* period sets in as the neophytes become aware that if there is a rush for liquidity prices will collapse. The race to move out of securities gathers pace.

7. Revulsion against securities develops as banks start calling in loans and selling collateral.

8. *Panic sets* in as the market collapses and the question arises as to whether the government or Central Bank should come in and act as a lender of last resort in what has been recently described as a "lifeboat operation."[10]

Help in accounting for how speculative bubbles are initiated comes to us from the Austrian School. The Austrian trade cycle theory serves to shed a bright light on how boom-bust business cycles are created, with speculative bubbles many times being an offshoot from these business-cycle booms.

The Austrian view of the trade cycle begins with the view that, in a market economy, entrepreneurs serve as forecasters, predicting what consumers will want in the future. After determining future wants, they set about the task of organizing and implementing the factors of production in the present, so that the product will be available when the consumers demand it, at a price sufficient for the entrepreneur to reap a profit.

What happens in a bust and the subsequent depression is that a preponderance of entrepreneurs have predicted in error and go bankrupt. Why is there this cluster of entrepreneurial errors? The answer lies not in examining the bust, but the boom that leads up to the crisis.

The boom-bust cycle begins with a monetary intervention into the economy. In the modern world, this occurs by way of the banking system's excessive issue of credit. This increase in what Mises called "fiduciary media," or unbacked banknotes or deposits, serves to reduce interest rates, and sends the false signal to entrepreneurs that consumers have changed their consumption/investment mix to one of greater investment and less consumption. Businessmen then invest this increased amount of money in capital goods, shifting resources away from consumer goods.

---

[10]Antoin Murphy, *Richard Cantillon: Entrepreneur and Economist* (Oxford: Clarendon Press, 1986), pp. 66–67; emphasis in original.

Prices and wages are then bid up in capital goods industries, but as this new money trickles down to consumers, their "time preferences," or consumption/investment mixes, have not actually changed, thus there is no increase in demand for the now abundant capital goods. The increased supply of unwanted capital goods, or malinvestment, must then be liquidated. This liquidation is then followed by a recession or depression, which is the economy's healing period, serving to reallocate the factors of production to more productive and efficient ways of satisfying customer wants.[11]

What also must be considered, when searching for what creates an environment from which speculative bubbles can emerge, is that age old question: What is the right amount of money for any given economy? Is more money beneficial for an economy? Does more money constitute more wealth? If more money is beneficial, then would not all the new money be channeled into production investment? David Hume explains what money is, and is not:

> Money is not, properly speaking, one of the subjects of commerce; but only the instrument which men have agreed upon to facilitate the exchange of one commodity for another. It is none of the wheels of trade: It is the oil which renders the motion of the wheels more smooth and easy.[12]

Money is useful only for its exchange-value, thus an increase in the supply of money, as Murray Rothbard indicates, *"does not—unlike other goods—confer a social benefit."*[13] Thus, if there is more money produced in an economy, its price will drop, making all other goods, which money is traded for, more expensive, in money terms.

---

[11]Murray Rothbard, *America's Great Depression*, 4th ed. (New York: Richardson & Snyder,1983), pp. 15–25.

[12]David Hume, *Writings on Economics*, Eugene Rotwein, ed., 2nd ed. (Madison: The University of Wisconsin Press, 1970), p. 33.

[13] Murray N. Rothbard, *What Has Government Done to Our Money?*, 4rd ed. (Auburn, Ala.: Ludwig von Mises Institute, 1990), p. 33; emphasis in original.

8 — *Early Speculative Bubbles and Increases in the Supply of Money*

The supply of money in the free market is determined by the market. So if gold is the money in a particular economy, the market will decide the amount of gold that will be produced for use as money. All of the gold that is mined will not be demanded by the market for use as money. Some of the precious metal would be channeled toward jewelry or industrial uses. But if by government mandate all gold is coined, even though the market does not demand it, the effect of this over-supply of money will lead to the same malinvestments as an increase in fiduciary media.[14]

Three different speculative bubbles will be explored in this volume. The first is Tulipmania, which occurred in 1634–37 in Amsterdam. The Tulipmania episode was spurred by the enormous influx of silver, and to a lesser extent, gold specie into Amsterdam. This influx was the result of free coinage laws, the stability of the Bank of Amsterdam, increased trade, and the Dutch Navy's success on the high seas at confiscating treasure.

Next, is a discussion about the life and theories of perhaps the world's first inflationist, John Law and the bubble that he directly engineered, the Mississippi Bubble. Law viewed paper money, and in fact stocks, bonds, or any other financial instruments as superior to gold or silver money. Law, like so many after him, also felt that low interest rates and more money were essential for a healthy, thriving economy. Law was to fuel the speculation in Mississippi Company shares with enormous amounts of banknotes before the house of paper finally collapsed. The South Sea Bubble, which occurred almost simultaneously with the Mississippi Bubble, was an attempt to mirror Law's system, refinancing government debt with the shares of the South Sea Company. This company, whose share price was to rise ten-fold, had no real assets and could only make a profit from a large increase in the price of its stock. The share price increase was aided with increased bank loans and other credit.

---

[14]F.A. Hayek, *A Free-Market Monetary System and The Pretense of Knowledge* (Auburn, Ala.: Ludwig von Mises Institute, 2008), pp. 12–15.

In conclusion, these three episodes shall be viewed in the context of the Austrian theory of malinvestment. What will also be considered are the prospects for the continued occurrence of speculative bubbles and the inevitable crashes that follow, given fiat banking and the presence of ubiquitous central banks waiting to prolong any boom and prop up any inevitable bust.

Tulipmania 2

"Tulipmania" has come to be virtually a metaphor in the economics field. When one looks up Tulipmania in *The New Palgrave Dictionary of Economics*, a discussion of the seventeenth century Dutch speculative mania will not be found. The author, Guillermo Calvo, instead defines tulipmania as: "situations in which some prices behave in a way that appears not to be fully explainable by economic 'fundamentals'."[1] Calvo then goes on to use mathematical models to discuss "equilibria that may resemble tulipmanias, but which are consistent with standard demand-supply analysis under the assumption of Perfect Foresight or Rational Expectations."

Brown University economist Peter Garber has written extensively about Tulipmania. Garber's article, "Tulipmania," sought to explore the fundamentals of the Amsterdam tulip market in 1634–37.[2] After a cursory review of the historical accounts of Tulipmania, centering for the most part on the seven pages Charles Mackay devoted to the subject in *Memoirs of Extraordinary Popular Delusions and the Madness of Crowds*, Garber initiates a discussion of

---

[1] Guillermo Calvo, "Tulipmania," in *The New Palgrave: A Dictionary of Economics,* John Eatwell, Murray Milgate, and Peter Newman, eds., 4 vols. (New York: The Stockton Press, 1987), p. 707

[2] Peter Garber, "Tulipmania," *Journal of Political Economy* 97, no. 3 (1989): 535–60.

the tulip and tulip markets of 1634 Holland. He begins by dispensing information on the nature of the tulip.

The tulip, being a bulb flower, can reproduce either by seed or through buds formed on female bulbs. The buds can reproduce another bulb if properly cultivated, the most effective method of reproduction being that of asexual reproduction through buds. The flowers of the tulip appear in April and May, and are only in bloom for about a week. The bulbs can be removed from the ground in June, but must be replanted again by September.

The extraordinary patterns some tulips display is caused by a mosaic virus. These patterns cannot be duplicated by seed reproduction; it is only by cultivating the effected buds into new bulbs that duplication can occur. The seeds produce only common flowers that later succumb to the virus creating new patterns. The downside to the virus is that it subdues the rate of reproduction. Thus, those tulips with more exotic patterns, were slower to reproduce, making them more scarce and valuable than common, uninfected bulbs.[3]

Garber's discussion of the bulb market begins with the assertion that this market was limited to professional growers until late 1634, when speculators entered the market, driven by high demand for bulbs in France. Rare bulbs were traded as "piece" goods by weight, with the weight standard being an aas, about one-twentieth of a gram. Common bulbs traded in standard units of 1,000 azen or one pound (9,728 azen in Haarlem, 10,240 azen in Amsterdam), with contracts not referring to specific bulbs.

Given the growing season mentioned above, the tulip market was a futures market from September to June. Garber indicates that formal futures markets began in 1636, and were the primary vehicle for trading in bulbs until February 1637, when the market collapsed.[4] In the summer of 1636, trading of futures took place in taverns, in groups called "colleges," with few rules restricting bidding

---

[3]Ibid., pp. 541–42.
[4]Ibid.

and fees. Buyers were required to put up a small fraction of the contracted amount of each deal for "wine money." Otherwise, Garber indicates, there was no margin required by either buyer or seller. On settlement date, buyers did not typically have the required cash to settle the trade, but the sellers did not have the bulbs to deliver either. Thus, the trade was settled with only a payment of the difference between the contract and settlement price being expected. Contracts were not repeatedly marked to the market; thus, when the market collapsed, gross positions, rather than net, had to be unwound.

With the market collapse in February 1637, no bulbs were delivered under the deals consummated by the new futures market. Bulbs could not be delivered until June. Garber says that it is unclear as to the settlement date and price for these transactions. It would appear that some sort of standard price was developed, based upon the price that the majority of trades settled at.

Rare bulbs began to trade at increasingly higher prices in 1635. However, it was November 1636 before the speculation in the common bulbs began. N.W. Posthumus said the following concerning the timing of events:

> I think the sequence of events may be seen as follows. At the end of 1634, the new non-professional buyers came into action. Towards the middle of 1635, prices rose rapidly, while people could buy on credit, generally delivering at once some article of value; at the same time the sale per aas was introduced. About the middle of 1636, the colleges appeared; and soon thereafter the trade in non-available bulbs was started, while in November of the same year the trade was extended to the common varieties, and bulbs were sold by the thousand azen and per pound.[5]

In the next section of Garber's "Tulipmania," he graphs price data for various types of bulbs, placing time on the horizontal axis (typically June 1636 through February 1637) and price (guilders or

---

[5]Quoted in ibid.

aas) on the vertical axis. All the graphs reflect sharply ascending slopes, at various degrees; six out of eight graphs reflect prices exploding upward to February 5, 1637 and plunging downward that same day. The graph for the Gouda bulb indicates its price peaked on January 29 and crashed on February 5 as with the other bulbs. The other graph, for the Semper Augustus bulb, reflects price information on a yearly scale and shows the peak price occurring in 1637.[6]

After the market crashed in the first week of February, a delegation of florists in Amsterdam on February 24th made the proposal that tulip sales contracts consummated before November 30, 1636 should be executed, but that transactions occurring after that date could be rescinded by the buyer upon payment of 10 percent of the sales price to the seller. However, the Dutch authorities came up with their own plan on April 27: to suspend all contracts. Thus, sellers could then sell contracted bulbs at the market prices during this suspension. Buyers were then responsible for the difference between this market price and the settlement price decided by the authorities. By doing this, growers were released to market bulbs to be exhumed that June. Garber goes on to explain that the disposition of further contracts is not clear, but the example of the city of Haarlem's solution is cited from Posthumus, which permitted buyers to cancel contracts upon payment of 3½ percent of the contract price.[7]

After a discussion of eighteenth-century tulip and hyacinth prices, along with modern bulb prices, Garber looks to answer the question: "Was This Episode a 'Tulipmania'?"[8] He responds to the issue that many works written about the economic history of seventeenth century Holland make just the slightest reference or no reference at all to Tulipmania by making the accurate point that, given the short duration of the mania, it had little effect on Holland's allocation of resources. Remember that bulbs must be planted by

---

[6]Ibid., pp. 543–45.
[7]Ibid., pp. 546–49.
[8]Ibid., pp. 547–50.

September and cannot be removed until June. Thus, at the apex of the bubble, November 1636 through January 1637, it was too late to plant more bulbs. Garber also contends that, in spite of the crash in tulip bulb prices, little wealth was transferred given that only small settlements were required on contracts.[9] This author questions this view that there was no financial pain felt from the crash. Other sources that will be explored later indicate that bankruptcies doubled in Amsterdam in 1637–38, a period immediately following the crash.

Garber comes to the conclusion that, "the bulb speculation was not obvious madness, at least for most of the 1634–37 "mania."[10] Only the last month of the speculation for common bulbs remains a potential bubble." Indeed, the price of the common bulb, the Witte Croonen, rose by approximately 26 times in January 1637, and subsequently fell to one-twentieth of its peak price the first week in February 1637.[11]

Economic historian Charles P. Kindleberger has written extensively on manias and bubbles. His book, *Manias, Panics, and Crashes: A History of Financial Crises*, is considered among the definitive books on the subject.[12] But Tulipmania, despite being a modern day metaphor for mania, is given but scant mention in a footnote, as follows:

> Manias such as the Lubeck crises 100 years earlier, or the tulip mania of 1634 are too isolated and lack the characteristic monetary features that come with the spread of banking after the opening of the eighteenth century. Peter Garber has dealt at length with the tulip mania. He distinguishes a "bubble" from ordinary economic fluctuations: the latter are determined by "fundamentals," while the former deviates from the set of prices that fundamentals would

---

[9]Ibid., pp. 555–56.

[10]Ibid., p. 558.

[11]Ibid., p. 556.

[12]Charles P. Kindleberger, *Manias, Panics, and Crashes: A History of Financial Crises* (New York: Basic Books, [1978] 1989).

call for. In the tulip mania, which he suggests was not a bubble, the fundamental accounting for the enormous rise of some tulip prices was the difficulty of producing them.[13]

In *A Financial History of Western Europe*, Kindleberger refers to tulip mania as "probably the high watermark in bubbles," yet only devotes five lines to the subject in the entire book.[14] Judging by his treatment of the subject, it would appear that Kindleberger, one of today's most noted mainstream economic historians, places little historical importance on the events in Amsterdam in 1634–37. The reason for Kindleberger's slight is found in the footnote referenced above, in particular: "lack the characteristic monetary features that come with the spread of banking in the eighteenth century." Kindleberger devotes chapter 4 of *Manias, Panics, and Crashes* to monetary expansion. He begins this chapter with the following:

> Speculative manias gather speed through expansion of money and credit or perhaps, in some cases, get started because of an initial expansion of money and credit. One can look back at particular manias followed by crashes or panics and see what went wrong.[15]

He then goes on to spend a couple of pages referencing various bubbles and ensuing crashes, all of which were created by monetary expansion.

However, Tulipmania is not mentioned for the obvious reason that Kindleberger does not believe that an expansion of the supply of money in Amsterdam created Tulipmania. Later in the same chapter, the Bank of Amsterdam is talked about. The bank, at the time of Tulipmania, did not perform credit operations, but only issued notes against deposits of specie. Thus, it's highly probable that, in Kindleberger's view, the supply of money did not undergo

---

[13]Ibid., p. 7.

[14]Charles Kindelberger, *A Financial History of Western Europe* (London: George Allen and Unwin, 1984), pp. 215, 272.

[15]Kindleberger, *Manias, Panics, and Crashes*, p. 57.

the sudden increase needed to create a speculative bubble. But in fact the supply of money in Amsterdam had increased dramatically, and that is where our story of Tulipmania begins.

Free Coinage, the Bank of Amsterdam, and Tulipmania 3

After the fall of the Roman Empire, many different money systems prevailed throughout Europe. Kings were eager to strike their own gold and silver coins. These coins were typically made full legal tender at a ratio of value fixed by the individual states. This supreme right of coinage was exercised and misused by every sovereign in Europe. After the fall of Byzantium, the sacred images which were struck on most coins disappeared. These sacred images had kept the superstitious masses, not to mention states, from altering the coins. But, without these sacred images, these gold and silver coins underwent numerous alterations, to the point where it was difficult to follow either a coin's composition or value. This "sweating," "clipping," or "crying" of coins continued right up to the beginning of the seventeenth century, with all of Europe's various rulers being guilty. These kings quickly found that an empty state treasury could be filled by debasing the currency.

The powerful Charles V was among the most culpable for altering the value of money. These alterations in the Netherlands came by monetary decree. In 1524, Charles raised the value of his gold coins from nine or ten, to eleven and three-eighths times their weight in silver coins. This created immense displeasure throughout the kingdom, so much that, in 1542, Charles returned to a ratio of ten to one, not by lowering the value of his gold coins back to their value before 1524, but by degrading his silver coins. Four years later, in 1546, Charles struck again, suddenly raising the value of his gold coins to thirteen times the value of silver coins. These actions served to first overvalue and then undervalue gold in relation to its market value to silver,[1] with the result being that the overvalued money drove the undervalued money out of circulation. This phenomenon is known as Gresham's Law. A silver ducat went from 54 grains fine down to 35 grains fine.[2] Thus, with silver coins being the primary circulating medium of Holland, this action reduced the value of the circulating money supply by one-third from its value in 1523, and raised the value of gold nearly 50 percent. By this device, Charles was able to replenish his dwindling treasury.

This transgression, in 1546, writes Del Mar, may have been "the straw that broke the patience of his long-suffering subjects."[3] A revolution was then sparked in the Netherlands, and, although Charles was able to check any upheaval during his reign, with the accession of Phillip the Bigot, the smoldering revolutionary fires burst into intense flames. After the "Confederation of Beggars" formed in 1566, six years later the revolution was proclaimed.

One of the first measures instigated by the revolutionary government was "Free" or "individual" coinage. Helfferich explains:

> The simplest and best-known special case of unrestricted transformation of a metal into money is that known as "the right of free coinage," or "coinage for private account." The

---

[1]The ratio of silver to gold from 1524 to 1546, based on the average for Europe, fluctuated between approximately 10½ and 11 (E.E. Rich and C.H. Wilson, eds., *The Cambridge Economic History of Europe*, vol. 4: *The Economy of Expanding Europe in the Sixteenth and Seventeenth Centuries* [Cambridge: Cambridge University Press, 1975], p. 459).

[2]Alexander Del Mar, *History of Monetary Systems: A Record of Actual Experiments in Money Made By Various States of the Ancient and Modern World, as Drawn From Their Statutes, Customs, Treaties, Mining Regulations, Jurisprudence, History, Archeology, Coins Nummulary Systems, and Other Sources of Information* (New York: Augustus Kelley Publishers, [1895] 1969), p. 345.

[3]Ibid., p. 348.

> State will mint coins out of any quantity of metal delivered to it, either making no charge to the person delivering the metal, or merely a very small charge to cover cost. The person delivering the metal receives in coin from the mint the quantity of the metal delivered up by him either without any deduction or with a very small deduction for seigniorage.[4]

The idea of free coinage was brought to the Netherlands from the Dutch East Indians, who inherited the concept from the Portuguese. The practice was originated by the degenerate Moslem governments of India, and was copied by Mascarenhas in 1555.[5]

Free coinage was an immediate success. Possessors of silver and gold bullion obtained in America,

> had vainly sought to evade the coinage exactions of the European princes; now the door of escape was open; they had only to be sent to Holland, turned into guilders and ducats, and credited as silver metal under the name of sols banco.[6]

As the seventeenth century began, the Dutch were the driving force behind European commerce. With Amsterdam as capital of Holland, it served as the central point of trade. Amsterdam's currency consisted primarily of the coins of the neighboring countries and, to a lesser extent, its own coins. Many of these foreign coins were worn and damaged, thus reducing the value of Amsterdam's currency about 9 percent below that of "the standard" or the legal tender. Thus, it was impossible to infuse any new coins into circulation. Upon the circulation of newly minted coins, these newly minted coins were collected, melted down and exported as bullion. Their place in circulation was quickly taken by newly imported "clipped" or "sweated" coins. Thus, undervalued money was driven

---

[4]Karl Helfferich, *Money*, Louis Infield, trans. (New York: Augustus M. Kelley, [1927] 1969), p. 370.

[5]Del Mar, *History of Monetary Systems*, pp. 344–51.

[6]Ibid., p. 351.

out by overvalued or degraded money, due to the legal tender status given these degraded coins.[7]

To remedy this situation, the Bank of Amsterdam was originated in 1609. The Bank was to facilitate trade, suppress usury, and have a monopoly on all trading of specie. But the bank's chief function was the withdrawal of abused and counterfeit coin from circulation.[8] Coins were taken in as deposits, with credits, known as bank money issued against these deposits, based not on the face value of the coins, but on the metal weight or intrinsic value of the coins. Thus, a perfectly uniform currency was created. This feature of the new money, along with its convenience, security and the City of Amsterdam's guarantee,[9] caused the bank money to trade at an agio, or premium over coins. The premium varied (4 to 6¼ percent), but generally represented the depreciation rate of coin below its nominal or face value.[10]

One of the services that the Bank provided was to transfer, upon order from a depositor, sums (deposits) to the account of creditors by book entry. This is called a giro banking operation. This service was so popular that the withdrawal of deposits from the bank became a very rare occurrence. If a depositor wanted to regain his specie, he could easily find a buyer for his bank money, at a premium, due to its convenience. Additionally, there was a demand for bank money from people not having an account with the Bank.[11] As

---

[7]Adam Smith, *An Inquiry into the Nature and Causes of the Wealth of Nations* (New York: Random House, [1776] 1965), p. 447.

[8]Herbert I. Bloom, *The Economic Activities of the Jews of Amsterdam in the Seventeenth and Eighteenth Centuries* (New York/London: Kennikat Press, [1937] 1969), pp. 172–73.

[9]The city of Amsterdam was bound for the coin or bullion's security while at the Bank, against fire, robbery, or any other accident.

[10]Richard Hildreth, *The History of Banks: To Which is Added, A Demonstration of the Advantages and Necessity of Free Competition in the Business of Banking* (New York: Augustus M. Kelley, [1837] 1968), p. 9.

[11]Shepard B. Clough, *European Economic History: The Economic Development of Western Civilization* (New York: McGraw-Hill, 1968), p. 199.

Adam Smith related in the *Wealth of Nations*: "By demanding payment of the bank, the owner of a bank credit would lose this premium."[12] The City of Amsterdam's guarantee, in addition to the requirement that all bills drawn upon or negotiated in Amsterdam, in the amount of six hundred guilders or more, must be paid in bank money, "took away all uncertainty in the value of the bills," and thus forced all merchants to keep an account at the bank, "which necessarily occasioned a certain demand for bank money."

Smith goes on to explain the mechanics of how the Bank of Amsterdam issued bank money.[13] The Bank would give credit (bank money) in its books for gold and silver bullion deposited, at roughly 5 percent below the bullion's then current mint value. At the same time as this bank credit was issued, the depositor would receive a receipt that entitled the depositor, or bearer, to draw the amount of bullion deposited from the bank, within six months of the deposit. Thus, to retrieve a bullion deposit, a person had to present to the bank: (1) a receipt for the bullion, (2) an amount of bank money equal to the book entry, and (3) payment of a ¼ percent fee for silver deposits, or ½ percent fee for gold deposits. Should the six month term expire with no redemption, or without payment of a fee to extend for an additional six months, "the deposit should belong to the bank at the price at which it had been received, or which credit had been given in the transfer books." Thus, the bank would make the 5 percent fee for warehousing the deposit, if it were not redeemed within the six-month time frame. The higher fee charged for gold was due to the fact that gold was thought to be riskier to warehouse, because of its higher value. A receipt for bullion was rarely allowed to expire. When it did happen, more often than not, it was a gold deposit because of its higher deposit fee.

This system created two separate instruments that were combined to create an obligation of the Bank of Amsterdam. As Smith explains:

---

[12]Smith, *An Inquiry into the Nature and Causes of the Wealth of Nations*, pp. 447–48.

[13]Ibid., pp. 448–49.

> The person who by making a deposit of bullion obtains both a bank credit and a receipt, pays his bills of exchange as they become due with his bank credit; and either sells or keeps his receipt according as he judges that the price of bullion is likely to rise or to fall. The receipt and the bank credit seldom keep long together, and there is no occasion that they should. The person who has a receipt, and who wants to take out bullion, finds always plenty of bank credits, or bank money to buy at ordinary price; and the person who has bank money, and wants to take out bullion, finds receipts always in equal abundance.
>
> The holder of a receipt cannot draw out the bullion for which it is granted, without re-assigning to the bank a sum of bank money equal to the price at which the bullion had been received. If he has no bank money of his own, he must purchase it of those who have it. The owner of bank money cannot draw out bullion without producing to the bank receipts for the quantity which he wants. If he has none of his own, he must buy them of those who have them. The holder of a receipt, when he purchases bank money, purchases the power of taking out a quantity of bullion, of which the mint price is 5 percent, above the bank price. The agio of 5 percent, therefore, which he commonly pays for it, is paid, not for an imaginary, but for the real value. The owner of bank money, when he purchases a receipt, purchases the power of taking out a quantity of bullion, of which the market price is commonly from 2 to 3 percent, above the mint price. The price which he pays for it, therefore, is paid likewise for a real value. The price of the receipt, and the price of the bank money, compound or make up between them the full value or price of the bullion.[14]

The same system that Smith describes above, also applied to coins that were deposited with the bank. Smith does assert that deposits of coinage were more likely to "fall to the bank" than deposits of bullion.[15] Due to the high agio (Smith indicates typically

---

[14]Ibid., p. 450.
[15]Ibid., p. 451.

5 percent) of bank money over common coin, the paying of the bank's six-month storage fee created a loss for holders of receipts.

The amount of bank money for which the receipts had expired, in relation to the total amount of bank money was very small. Smith writes:

> The bank of Amsterdam has for these many years past been the great warehouse of Europe for bullion, for which the receipts are very seldom allowed to expire or, as they express it, to fall to the bank. The far greater part of the bank money, or of the credits upon the books of the bank, is supposed to have been created, for these many years past, by such deposits which the dealers in bullion are continually both making and withdrawing.[16]

The bank was highly profitable for the city of Amsterdam. Besides the aforementioned warehouse rent and sale of bank money for the agio, each new depositor paid a fee of ten guilders to open an account. Any subsequent account opened by that depositor would be subject to a fee of three guilders. Transfers were subject to a fee of two guilders, except when the transfer was for less than six hundred guilders. Then the fee was six guilders (to discourage small transfers). Depositors were required to balance their accounts twice a year. If the depositor failed to do this, he incurred a twenty-five guilder penalty. A fee of 3 percent was charged if a depositor ordered a transfer for more than the amount of his account.[17]

In the beginning, the Bank of Amsterdam did not perform a credit function; it was strictly a deposit bank, with all bank money backed 100 percent by specie. The administration of the Bank of Amsterdam was the charge of a small committee of city government officials. This committee kept the affairs of the bank secret. Because of the secretive nature of its administration, it was not generally known that individual depositors had been allowed to overdraw their accounts as early as 1657. In later years, the Bank also began

---

[16]Ibid., p. 451.
[17]Ibid., p. 454.

to make large loans to the Dutch East India Company and the Municipality of Amsterdam. By 1790 word of these loans became public and the premium on bank money (usually 4 percent, but sometimes as high as 6¼ percent) disappeared and fell to a 2 percent discount. By the end of that year, the Bank virtually admitted insolvency by issuing a notice that silver would be sold to holders of bank money at a 10 percent discount. The City of Amsterdam took over the Bank in 1791 and eventually closed it for good in December of 1819.[18]

The effects of free coinage, combined with the stability of the Bank of Amsterdam, created the impetus that channeled the large amounts of precious metals being discovered in America, and to a lesser degree in Japan, towards the direction of Amsterdam.

After Columbus came to America in 1492 and Cortés invaded Mexico in 1519, an influx of precious metals into Europe began, principally through Spain. The output of these fertile mines in the Americas reversed a trend of lower prices in Europe that had been caused by the combination of static metals production in Europe and rapidly expanding industry and commerce. Production in the New World was further increased after the discovery of Peru's Huancavelica mercury mine in 1572. The amalgamation process which was invented in the mid-sixteenth century depended heavily on mercury. This process greatly increased the efficiency of the silver production process.[19]

The Japanese silver-mining industry was also expanding at the same time, but without the benefit of the mercury-amalgam process. The Dutch East India Company had a virtual monopoly on trade with Japan and, of course, access to their precious metals production from 1611 through the end of the century. Del Mar points out that, "from 1624 to 1853 the Dutch were the only Europeans permitted

---

[18]Charles Arthur Conant, *History of Modern Banks of Issue* (New York: Augustus M. Kelley Publishers, [1927] 1969), p. 289.

[19]Hamilton, Earl J. "Imports of American Gold and Silver into Spain, 1503–1660," *Quarterly Journal of Economics* 43 (1929): 436–43.

to trade with Japan," managing "to obtain about one-half of the total exports of the precious metals from Japan."[20]

Flynn indicates that:

> American output of bullion, in conjunction with the output of Central European and Japanese mines, increased the world's supply of silver sufficiently to slowly drive its market value downward. That is, there was price inflation in the sixteenth century. American and non-American mines produced such an enormous quantity of silver that its market value dropped to a level below the cost of producing it in a growing number of European mines.[21]

Francis Amasa Walker validates this view: "the astonishing production of silver at Potosi began to be felt. From 1570 to 1640 silver sank rapidly. Corn rose from about two oz. of silver the quarter, to six or eight oz."[22] Walker goes on to quote David Hume:

> By the most exact computations that have been formed all over Europe, after making allowance for the alterations in the numerary value, or the denomination, it is found that the prices of all things have risen three, four, times since the discovery of the West Indies.[23]

Table 1 illustrates this large influx of precious metals.

Bullion flowed from Spain to Amsterdam due to both trade and seizure of treasure. As Violet Barbour relates:

> In 1628 occurred the famous capture of the Spanish treasure fleet by Piet Heyn, which netted 177,537 lbs. weight of silver, besides jewels and valuable commodities, the total

---

[20]Alexander Del Mar, *A History of the Precious Metals, from the Earliest Times to the Present* (New York: Augustus M. Kelley, [1902] 1969), pp. 307–08.

[21]Dennis O. Flynn, "Sixteenth-Century Inflation from a Production Point of View," in *Inflation Through The Ages: Economic, Social, Psychological and Historical Aspects*, Nathan Schmukler and Edward Marcus, eds. (New York: Brooklyn College Press, 1983), p. 162, 164.

[22]Francis Amasa Walker, *Money* (New York: Augustus M. Kelley, [1881] 1968), p. 135.

[23]Ibid.

estimated to come to 11 1/2 to 15 million florins. More important than such occasional windfalls was the share of Dutch merchants in the new silver brought twice a year to Cadiz from the mines of Mexico and Peru, a share which represented in part the profits of trade with Spain and through Spain with the New World. Just what that share was from year to year we do not know. Only a few fragmentary estimates for non-consecutive years in the second half

TABLE 1
SPANISH IMPORTS OF FINE GOLD AND SILVER FROM AMERICA
(IN GRAMS)

PERIOD	SILVER	GOLD
1503–1510		4,965,180
1511–1520		9,153,220
1521–1530	148,739	4,889,050
1531–1540	86,193,876	14,466,360
1541–1550	177,573,164	24,957,130
1551–1560	303,121,174	42,620,080
1561–1570	942,858,792	11,530,940
1571–1580	1,118,591,954	9,429,140
1581–1590	2,103,027,689	12,101,650
1591–1600	2,707,626,528	19,541,420
1601–1610	2,213,631,245	11,764,090
1611–1620	2,192,255,993	8,855,940
1621–1630	2,145,339,043	3,889,760
1631–1640	1,396,759,594	1,240,400
1641–1650	1,056,430,966	1,549,390
1651–1660	443,256,546	469,430
TOTAL	16,866,815,303	181,333,180

Source: Earl J. Hamilton, *American Treasure and the Price Revolution in Spain* (Cambridge, Mass.: Harvard University Press, 1934), reprinted in Shepard B. Clough, *European Economic History: The Economic Development of Western Civilization* (New York: McGraw-Hill, 1968), p. 150.

of the century have come to light. According to these the Dutch usually carried off from 15 to 25 percent of the treasure brought by the galleons and the flota, their share sometimes exceeding, sometimes falling below the amounts claimed by France or Genoa.[24]

Del Mar echoes this view:

> The honest Abbe Raynal explains the whole matter in a few words: whilst the Portuguese robbed the Indians, the Dutch robbed the Portuguese. "In less than half a century the ships of the Dutch East India Company took more than three hundred Portuguese vessels laden with the spoils of Asia. These brought the Company immense returns." Much of eastern gold, which found its way to Amsterdam was proceeds of double robbery.[25]

Further evidence of an exceptionally large increase in the supply of money in the Netherlands is provided in table 2.

TABLE 2
TOTAL MINT OUTPUT OF THE SOUTH NETHERLANDS, 1598–1789
(IN GUILDERS)

PERIOD	GOLD	SILVER	COPPER	TOTAL
1628–29	153,010	2,643,732	4,109	2,800,851
1630–32	364,414	8,838,411	6,679	9,209,503
1633–35	476,996	16,554,079		17,031,075
1636–38	2,917,826	20,172,257		23,090,083
1639–41	2,950,150	8,102,988		11,053,138
1642–43	2,763,979	1,215,645	47,834	4,027,458

Source: Jan A. van Houtte and Leon van Buyten, "The Low Countries" in *An Introduction to the Sources of European Economic History 1500–1800*, Charles Wilson and Geoffrey Parker, eds. (Ithaca, N.Y.: Cornell University Press, 1977), p. 100.

---

[24]Violet Barbour, *Capitalism in Amsterdam in the 17th Century* (Ann Arbor: University of Michigan Press, 1963), pp. 49–50.

[25]Del Mar, *A History of the Precious Metals*, pp. 326–27.

30 — *Early Speculative Bubbles and Increases in the Supply of Money*

The numbers in table 2 point to the explosive increase in the supply of money for the time period from 1630–38, during the later part of which Tulipmania took place (1634–37).

Figure 1 shows the deposits in the Bank of Amsterdam. An exceptional growth in deposits is reflected for the period from

FIGURE 1
DEPOSITS IN THE BANK OF AMSTERDAM, 1625–1650

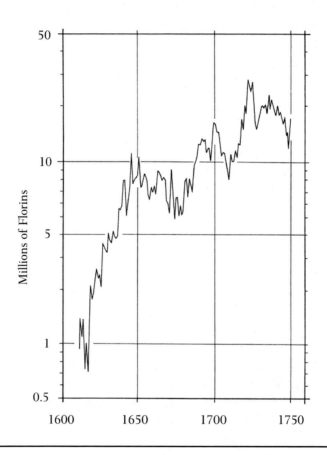

Source: J.G. van Dillen, reprinted in Frank C. Spooner, *The International Economy and Monetary Movements in France, 1493–1725* (Harvard Economic Studies, vol. 138; Cambridge, Mass.: Harvard University Press, 1972), p. 68.

approximately 1625 to 1650. Upon close inspection it appears that from the year 1633 to 1638 deposits grew from five million florins to eight million florins, a 60 percent increase!

As the above evidence indicates, free coinage, the Bank of Amsterdam, and the heightened trade and commerce in Holland served to attract coin and bullion to Amsterdam from throughout the world. As Del Mar writes:

> Under the stimulus of "free" coinage, an immense quantity of the precious metals now found their way to Holland, and a rise of prices ensued, which found one form of expression in the curious mania of buying tulips at prices often exceeding that of the ground on which they were grown.[26]

Del Mar goes on to discuss the end of Tulipmania:

> In 1648, when the Peace of Westphalia acknowledged the independence of the Dutch republic, the latter stopped the "free" coinage of silver florins and only permitted it for gold ducats, which in Holland had no legal value. This legislation discouraged the imports of silver bullion, checked the rise of prices, and put an end to the tulip mania.[27]

Del Mar concedes in a footnote that the mania had already been discouraged on April 27th, 1637 by a resolution of the States-General that canceled all contracts.

The crash of tulip prices left the growers of the bulbs to absorb the majority of the financial damage of the mania. With the government basically canceling all contracts, growers could not find new buyers or recover money owed them by buyers supposedly under contract. As Simon Schama describes:

> In any event, the magistrates of the Dutch towns saw niceties of equity as less pressing than the need to de-intoxicate the tulip craze. Their intervention was hastened by the urgency of returning the genie speculation to the bottle from which it had escaped, and corking it tightly to ensure

---

[26]Del Mar, *History of Monetary Systems*, p. 351.

[27]Ibid., p. 352.

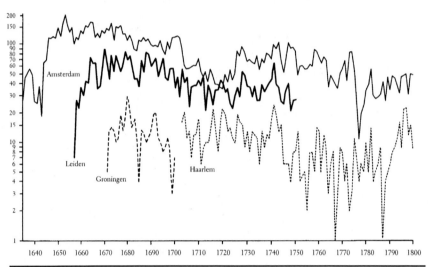

Source: Charles Wilson and Geoffrey Parker, eds., *An Introduction to the Sources of European Economic History 1500–1800* (Ithaca, N.Y.: Cornell University Press, 1977), p. 102.

against any recurrence. To some extent, they could feel satisfied that the ineluctable operations of Fortuna had already punished the foolhardy by taking them from rags to riches and back again in short order. But they still felt impelled to launch a didactic campaign in tracts, sermons and prints against folly, since its special wickedness had been in leading the common people astray.[28]

In spite of the short duration of the tulip craze and assertions by other authors to the contrary, there is evidence of financial pain that resulted from tulipmania. Figure 2 depicts the number of annual bankruptcies in Amsterdam, Leiden, Haarlem and Groningen from 1635–1800, presented by Messrs. van Houtte and van Buyten, reflects a doubling in the number in Amsterdam from 1635

---

[28]Simon Schama, *The Embarrassment of Riches* (New York: Alfred A. Knopf, 1987), pp. 361–62.

to 1637.[29] It would be hard to imagine that only tulip growers made up this increase in the number of bankruptcies. I suspect some of the "foolhardy masses" were among this group.

The story of Tulipmania is not only about tulips and their price movements, and certainly studying the "fundamentals of the tulip market" does not explain the occurrence of this speculative bubble. The price of tulips only served as a manifestation of the end result of a government policy that expanded the quantity of money and thus fostered an environment for speculation and malinvestment. This scenario has been played out over and over throughout history. But what made this situation unique was that the government policy did not expand the supply of money through fractional-reserve banking, which is the modern tool. Actually, it was quite the opposite that occurred. As kings throughout Europe debased their currencies, through clipping, sweating, or by decree, the Dutch provided a sound currency policy which called for money to be backed 100 percent by specie. This policy, combined with the occasional seizure of bullion and coin from Spanish ships on the high seas, served to attract coin and bullion from throughout the world. The end result was a large increase in the supply of coin and bullion in 1630s Amsterdam. Free coinage laws then served to create more money from this increased supply of coin and bullion than what the market demanded. This acute increase in the supply of money served to foster an atmosphere that was ripe for speculation and malinvestment, which manifested itself in the intense trading of tulips.

The Bank of Amsterdam, and the bank money it issued, served as the inspiration for John Law's early theories on money. The early seventeenth-century episode in Holland, known as Tulipmania, was not only a bubble, driven by the same monetary features as later bubbles, but its catalyst, The Bank of Amsterdam, served to inspire the man who was to create two later (and more famous) bubbles, the Mississippi and South Sea Bubbles.

---

[29]Jan A. Van Houtte and Leon Van Buyten, "The Low Countries" in *An Introduction to the Sources of European Economic History 1500–1800* (Ithaca, N.Y.: Cornell University Press, 1977), p. 102.

John Law, Genius or Swindler 4

Perhaps no person in the history of economics has inspired such strong opinions, both for and against, as John Law. Some view Law as a genius. To others he is considered a madman and swindler. In many ways, he was all of these things.

Very rarely is an economist presented with the opportunity that John Law enjoyed. Typically, the closest an economist comes to implementing his or her ideas is by serving in some advisory capacity to a ruler, president, or governing body. But even in this capacity, the economist's recommendation becomes just one of many considerations that the politician or monarch takes under advisement when setting economic policies. But Law's situation was much different. Law himself said, after his fall, that he had exercised more power than any other uncrowned individual in Europe. At the height of his power, he controlled the Royal Bank (and thus the supply of money), the public debt, indirect taxes, colonial trade, the tobacco monopoly, and more than half of what is now the continental United States. Additionally, Law was the finance minister, the main economic advisor, and the favorite of an absolute prince.[1]

---

[1] Earl J. Hamilton, "Law, John" in *International Encyclopedia of the Social Sciences*, David L. Sills, ed. (New York: Macmillan and The Free Press, 1968), p. 80.

Because of his power, Law was able to manipulate all aspects of the French economy, and gave what is now known as "Keynesian economics" its first test. Ultimately, Law's system ended in disaster. But unfortunately, the mistakes made by John Law and his imitators in Britain continue to be made over and over again, to this day.

John Law was born in Edinburgh in 1671, the son of a goldsmith-banker. Law's father died when John was in his teens.[2] Law's mother, a distant relative of the Duke of Argyll, saw to it that her son received an education in both theoretical and applied economics. Mackay indicates that young John worked for his father for three years, learning the Scottish banking trade. Law displayed a great aptitude for numbers, which aided in his quick grasp of the principles of the banking business.

After the death of his father, Law's interest in the banking business waned. At age seventeen, Law was a strapping young man who was a favorite with the ladies, in spite of his face being deeply scarred from the small-pox. The young women called him Beau Law, while the men nicknamed him Jessamy John, for his foppery.

With young Law receiving an inheritance from his father's estate, he could afford to take off and see the world. His first stop was London, which provided John the opportunity to profit from certain gambling systems using his considerable mathematics skills. Law was the envy of all the other gamblers, who after witnessing his success, began to follow his bets. Law's way with the ladies continued in London, with John having his choice of the most beautiful.

Law's life of leisure continued for nine years. But by this time, John was addicted to gambling, and he eventually lost more than he could repay without mortgaging his family estate. About this same time, Law's love life also created trouble. While in London, a love affair with Elizabeth Villiers,[3] led to a duel with a jealous suitor of

---

[2]Hamilton indicates that Law's father died when John was age 13, Mackay indicates that Law was 17. See Charles Mackay, *Memoirs of Extraordinary Popular Delusions and the Madness of Crowds* (London: Richard Bentley, New Burlington Street, [1841] 1963), p. 3.

[3]Later she became the Countess of Orkney.

Ms. Villiers, named Edward Wilson. Law proved to be good with a gun also, killing Wilson on the spot. Normally, this would not have been considered a grave offense. However, Wilson had many powerful friends, which, combined with the fact that Law was a foreigner, led to arrest on a charge of murder. After being found guilty, he was sentenced to death. But the sentence was subsequently lowered to just a fine on the grounds that his offense was only manslaughter. While being detained pending an appeal by Wilson's brother, Law bribed a guard and escaped to the continent. A reward was offered for him. Mackay quotes the ad in the *Gazette*, describing Law:

> Captain John Law, a Scotchman, aged twenty-six; a very tall, black, lean man; well shaped, above six-feet high, with large pock-holes in his face; big nosed, and speaking broad and loud.[4]

Mackay speculates that this description was published to aid Law in his escape, given its exaggerated nature. Law traveled for three years on the European continent studying the monetary and banking matters of the countries he was in by day, and speculating at the gaming tables by night.

After returning to Edinburgh in 1700, Law began to write on the subjects of money and trade. His first pamphlet entitled, *Proposals and Reasons for constituting a Council of Trade* was not well received.

Law went back to the continent after his proposal was sacked. More importantly, Law was unable to obtain a pardon for his murder of Mr. Wilson, thus making life in Scotland somewhat uncomfortable. For fourteen years, Law gambled his way across Europe, supporting himself on gaming wins. He was known in gambling halls everywhere as a skilled player. His reputation was such that he was *persona non grata*, in Venice and Genoa. The magistrates in those two cities believed him to be a dangerous influence on youth. While in Paris, Law made an enemy of the lieutenant-general of the police, who eventually told Law to leave town. However, by that

---

[4]Mackay, *Memoirs of Extraordinary Popular Delusions,* pp. 3–4.

time, Law had become friends with the Duke de Vendome, the Prince de Conti, and, more importantly, the Duke of Orléans. The Duke of Orléans and Law shared the preference for social life, and they frequently ran into each other at social functions. It was through the Duke of Orléans that Law would eventually implement his monetary and financial plans.[5]

Law submitted a proposal for a privately owned Bank of France to Madame de Maintenon, the head mistress of Louis XIV, in 1702. Part of the introduction of this proposal included the financial instruments that Law considered part of the money supply: stock in the Dutch and English East India companies, exchequer notes, Dutch government bonds, and Bank of England stock. Branches of the bank would be located in each province, with notes payable to bearer being redeemed at the parent bank in Paris or at any branch. Through this bank, Law argued, the supply of money could be increased, which would lower interest rates and stimulate economic activity. But the proposal was not accepted, some believe, due to Law's protestant faith, Louis being a catholic.[6]

With Scotland in the throes of a depression in 1704, the Bank of Scotland suspended specie payments. This development led Law, who was back in Edinburgh at the time, to make his land bank proposal to the Scottish Parliament. In 1705, this proposal was published anonymously as: *Money and Trade Considered: With a Proposal for Supplying the Nation With Money*. Numerous other tracts were written during that same period, with each author claiming that a lack of money was the cause of the crisis. Law's work, however, went much further than the others in terms of formulating the theory behind his proposal. But again, his work was for naught. In spite of

---

[5]Ibid., pp. 2–4.

[6]Both Mackay and Hamilton make reference to this religious bigotry. Mackay, *Memoirs of Extraordinary Popular Delusions,* p. 5, relates, "The reason given for the refusal is quite consistent with the character of that bigoted and tyrannical monarch." He also indicates that it has appeared in the correspondence of the Duchess of Orléans, Madame de Baviere, and the mother of the Regent.

support from the Lord High Commissioner, the Earl of Islay, and the Duke of Argyll, only two Scottish Parliament members supported the plan.[7]

In 1706, Law again was in France submitting his "Treatise on Money and Commerce" to French finance minister, Michel Chamillart. Hamilton calls this presentation Law's best, although it has never been published. Law was told to leave France due to his radical ideas, according to Hamilton, who argues that allegations that Law was banished because of his gambling prowess are untrue.[8]

Law's next stop was Italy, where, in 1711, he presented his bank proposal, based upon the Bank of England, to Vittorio Amadeo II, Duke of Savoy. Although impressed with Law's intelligence and knowledge, the Duke felt the plan much too ambitious for his small country. He urged Law to try the king of France again.[9]

France's new finance minister, Desmaretz, turned down Law's proposal yet again in July 1715. Desmaretz liked the plan, but was uneasy about a bank being so dominated by one man, especially if that man was to be John Law. But later that same year, persistence would finally pay off. Louis XIV died, and with the immediate heir to the throne being only seven years old, Law's old friend, the Duke of Orléans, assumed the reins of the French government.

Louis had made a shambles of the finances of the country. France was deeply in debt and on the verge of bankruptcy. The regent tried such odious tactics as a recoinage, which depreciated the currency by 20 percent, and aggressive, heavy handed attempts at increasing tax collections. Neither of these tactics worked. Rather, they served to incite the ire of the populace. Thus, when Law presented, his plan he was well received. But while Law was able to garner the Duke's support for a royal bank, the Council of Finance rejected the proposal on October 24, 1715. However, this was to be Law's last defeat. Law altered the plan, making the bank a privately

---

[7]Hamilton, "Law, John," p. 79.
[8]Ibid., p. 79.
[9]Mackay, *Memoirs of Extraordinary Popular Delusions*, pp. 5–6.

owned institution, and obtained a charter for the General Bank in early May, 1716.[10] Being the first Bank of France, Law was able to draft the charter document, and subscribed to 25 percent of its stock. Alas, Desmaretz's worst fears had come true, as the bank was completely dominated by Law, possibly more than any bank had or ever would be dominated by one man in history.[11]

---

[10]Hamilton indicates the 2nd of May, Mackay the 5th.
[11]Hamilton, "Law, John," p. 79.

John Law's Monetary Theories 5

John Law's *Money and Trade Considered With A Proposal For Supplying The Nation With Money* was published in 1705, and submitted to the Parliament of Scotland as a solution to lift that country from the depths of a depression. Law's solution, of course, was to create more money.

Law felt that the use of banks was the best method to increase the quantity of money. He was especially impressed with the Bank of Amsterdam and noted its contribution to the prowess of the Dutch in their trade and commercial endeavors, despite having no more natural advantages than his native Scotland. Law noted that the Bank of Amsterdam was a "secure place," and describes its original intent:

> Banks where the Money is pledg'd equal to the Credit given, are sure; For, tho Demands are made of the whole, the Bank does not fail in payment.[1]

Law goes on to say that unbacked credit was issued despite the constitution of this bank requiring 100 percent backing.

> Yet a Sum is lent by the Managers for a stock to the Lumbar, and 'tis thought they lend great sums on other occasions. So far as they lend they add to the money, which brings a Profit

---

[1] John Law, *Money and Trade Considered With A Proposal For Supplying The Nation With Money* (New York: Augustus M. Kelley, [1705] 1966), p. 37.

to the Country, by imploying more People, and extending Trade; They add to the Money to be lent, whereby it is easier borrowed, and at less use, and tho none suffer by it, or are apprehensive of Danger, its Credit being good; Yet if the whole Demands were made, or Demands greater than the remaining Money, they could not all be satisfied, till the Bank had called in what Sums were lent.[2]

Law then proposes that the conveniences to be gained from unreserved or unbacked money were more than equal to the risks involved.[3] Those conveniences being: less interest, more money, and ease of payments.

In *Money and Trade*, Law, although advocating a system of fractional-reserve banking, was not ignorant of its harmful effects:

Raising [debasing] the Money in *France* is laying a Tax on the People, which is sooner pay'd, and thought to be less felt than a Tax laid on any other way. . . . This Tax falls heavy on the poorer sort of the People.[4]

In the last half of *Money and Trade*, Law espouses his proposal for paper money backed by land, his view being that silver was unsuitable to be money because more and more of it was being produced. Thus, it became less valuable over time. Law believed that land would increase in value over time, for the following reasons: demand for it increases, improvements are made making it more productive, it does not lose any of its uses, and the amount stays the same. The following capsulizes Law's proposal:

The Paper-money propos'd will be equal in value to Silver, for it will have a value of Land pledg'd, equal to the same Sum of Silver-money, that it is given out for. If any Losses should happen, one 4th of the Revenue of the Commission, will in all appearance be more than sufficient to make them good.

---

[2]Ibid.
[3]Ibid., p. 41.
[4]Ibid., p. 51.

This Paper-money will not fall in value as Silver-money has fallen, or may fall: Goods or Money fall in value, if they increase in Quantity, or if the Demand lessens. But the Commission giving out what Sums are demanded, and taking back what Sums are offer'd to be return'd; This Paper-money will keep its value, and there will always be as much Money as there is occasion, or imployment for, and no more.[5]

Law lists the qualities necessary in money as being:

1. Ease of delivery
2. Same value everywhere
3. Kept without loss or expense
4. Divisible without loss
5. Capable of a stamp
6. Stable quantity[6]

Law insists that paper money has more of these qualities than silver. But should Law have been comparing the merits of silver vs. paper or of silver vs. land? If the paper money was to be backed by land, could one redeem their paper for land? If so, land itself must pass the above tests. If not, fiat paper must pass muster.

The following is Professor Murray Rothbard's necessary qualities for money:

1. Generally marketable (non-monetary value)
2. Divisible
3. High value per unit weight (portable)
4. Fairly stable supply
5. Durable
6. Recognizable
7. Homogeneous[7]

The two lists are similar, however, Rothbard's being somewhat more rigorous, it will be used for the comparison between silver, paper and land for use as money.

---

[5]Ibid., p. 89.

[6]Ibid., p. 93.

[7]Murray Rothbard, "History of Economic Thought," lecture at the University of Nevada at Las Vegas (Fall 1990).

TABLE 3

Quality	Silver	Paper	Land
1. non-monetary value	yes	no	yes
2. divisible	yes	yes	no
3. portable	yes	yes	no
4. stable supply	yes	no	yes
5. durable	yes	no	yes
6. recognizable	yes	no	yes
7. homogeneous	yes	yes	no

As table 3 reflects, silver passes the test with flying colors. Paper and land do not do as well. When looking at the paper and land columns, what stands out is that by merging these two columns, the three "no" qualities of land could be changed to "yeses" by paper, and the four paper "noes" can be changed to "yeses" by land. It's doubtful that Law went through this exercise, but his thought process must have been similar. However, the two cannot be merged. Paper backed by land would have to be redeemable in land. That forces land into the qualities of money test, with a predictable outcome.

Although Law spends 120 pages touting land-backed money in *Money and Trade*, this author believes that Law never intended that paper money would be redeemable in land. He was only attempting to build a case for paper money that would eventually have little or no backing. Law began to move toward this direction in later writings. He moved away from land and toward paper assets as backing for money, or to serve as money.

Antoin Murphy has written that Law, between 1707 and 1711, moved away from land bank proposals toward financial institutions patterned after the Bank of England and the East India Company. Instead of land backing financial claims, Law began to see the support being provided by:

> government securities and loans to the private sector, in the case of the Bank of England, to fixed and working capital

(ships, trading forts, harbours, stock in hand) and government securities in the case of the East India Company.[8]

In the late seventeenth and early eighteenth centuries, England was waging numerous wars, which it financed with continuous borrowing. This debt took the form of the government securities shown on the balance sheets of the Bank of England and the East India Company. The Bank, the East India Company, and later the South Sea Company, all were granted increased monopoly privileges in either banking or trading for their parts in buying up government debt at lower interest rates.

Through his interest in the Bank of England and the East India Company, Law expanded his view of what forms money could take. As early as 1707, only two years after *Money and Trade* was published, Law began to view exchequer bills, bills of exchange and tallies as money. In addition, new money was being created in the form of shares of stock in the Bank of England and East India Company. Murphy relates the following quote from Law in *"Mémoire pour prouver qu'une nouvelle espèce de monnaie peut être meilleure que l'or et 1 argent"*:

> What approximates most to a new type of money is the East India Company. The stock of this Company is divided into shares like that of the bank. They are traded each day on the exchange and the current price is published for the public's information in the gazettes. As the transfer of these shares is easy they are given and received in payment at the price at which they are traded, so that the merchant or trader with payments to make does not need to hold money as a reserve. As part of his capital is held in the Indies Company he can use these shares for payment and if difficulties in exchanging them at that day's market rate all he has to do is send them to the Exchange and convert them into specie, but as they are convertible they will not be refused.[9]

---

[8]"The Evolution of John Law's Theories and Policies 1707–1715," *European Economic Review* 34 (August 1991): 1113.

[9]Ibid., p. 1114.

Law believed that this "new" money would rise in value along with inflation, as opposed to silver specie that would decline in value as more was discovered or produced. Law felt that the exchequer bills and bills of exchange, like silver, were subject to this decline in value, because ultimately these instruments would be liquidated for specie. But Law was beginning to view shares of stock the way he had viewed land, as being superior to silver, believing that these shares could never decrease in value.

In *"Mémoire,"* Law continued to propose a banking system based upon his land-bank proposal. However, on a theoretical level, he was beginning to place more emphasis on liquidity. Murphy writes:

> He was defining as money any financial instrument that could be used as a medium of exchange. Tallies, exchequer bills and bills of exchange were used for facilitating exchange and so came to be regarded as money by Law.[10]

These *"les credits,"* however, still lacked an attribute that Law was looking for in money: being inflation proof. Thus, in Law's mind, the shares fit the bill, providing the superior store of value function that he was looking for. The capital of the East India Company was employed in productive activities, not just money, which provided this inflation protection. Law wanted his monetary system to be tied to productive assets. That was the case with his land-bank proposal—currency being backed by the productivity of the land—but now he was extending this idea to the capital of companies.

The shares of these companies were interpreted as media of exchange because of their ready marketability and, in Law's view, a view that tended to dismiss the downside risk associated with shares, were superior stores of value than money because they were linked to a productive capital base.[11]

In 1711, Law was in Italy advising the Duke of Savoy and preparing a proposal for a bank to be established in that country. The proposal was heavily influenced by the structure of the Bank of

---

[10]Ibid., p. 1115.

[11]Ibid., p. 1116.

England. Law, by that time, had dropped the land-bank plan, and was concentrating on a proposal that would incorporate the shares of the Bank of England and the East India Company into the supply of money. The Bank of England impressed Law for two reasons: its ability to finance the long and costly wars England was engaged in, and the way it had expanded the supply of money so that trade continued to expand in the face of the outflow of specie to finance the War of Spanish Succession. Murphy quotes Law from an unpublished manuscript in the *Archivio di Stato* in Turin, which Law wrote and sent to Amadeus, Duke of Savoy:

> The stock of the Indies Company is also divided up in shares, like that of the Bank. They are negotiated and received in payment. A merchant with payments to make does not keep large sums in cash. He invests a part of his capital in the Indies Company or in the Bank and gives this shareholding in payment when he has insufficient cash. If there are difficulties with respect to acceptance he sends them to the stock exchange to convert them into specie, but as they are negotiable they are not refused at the current market price. Most people prefer them to specie because no return is derived from specie until the occasion arises to use it. Shares constitute a value already in use which is productive.[12]

Law viewed France's problem in 1715 as twofold, a monetary crisis (too little money), similar to that of Scotland in 1705, and also a financial crisis, which stemmed from excessive war debts. Law sought to solve this problem by establishing a sinking fund to pay off a portion of the government debt and establish a bank to increase the supply of money. The bank was to be a joint venture between Law and the King, who would receive 75 percent of the profits. Law, in turn, would receive 25 percent. However, Law's plan called for the King's profits to be consigned to repaying France's debt. Thus, both problems would be served: the bank to meet the shortage of money and the king's profits to pay off the national debt. Law was linking monetary policy with financial policy.

---

[12]Unpublished manuscript in the *Archivio di Stato* in Turin, Italy. Mazzo J3 2a Categoria, p. 62. Quoted in ibid., p. 1117.

Law continued to develop this linkage in the "*Mémoire sur les Banques*," which was presented to the French authorities in July 1715. Law recommended a credit creating bank that issued banknotes, like the Bank of England. Law also reminded the authorities of the benefits of including bank shares as part of the media of exchange. Bank of England shares at that time were trading at a 30 premium over their par value. Law's proposal also included using bank profits to purchase the Hotel de Soissons, later to be used as the site for a stock exchange, the bank and a center for foreign-exchange transactions.[13]

Although he was repeatedly rejected by the French authorities, Law continued to write letters to the Regent espousing his grandiose plans. These plans began to include more than just his bank. Murphy quotes Law in a letter to the Regent as saying:

> But the bank is not the only nor the biggest of my ideas—I will produce a work which will surprise Europe by the changes that it will generate in France's favour, changes which will be greater than those produced by the discovery of the Indies or by the introduction of credit.[14]

From all appearances, this "work" Law was referring to was the inclusion of shares in the supply of money. Law wrote,

> I will lighten the burden of the King and the State in lowering the rate of interest on money, not by legal methods, but by an abundance of specie.[15] The specie which France mints from bullion taken from the Indies falls and loses its value in accordance with the quantities brought into Europe—the credit which I propose to introduce will have a more assured value and will gain 20 and 30 percent on specie.[16]

It is clear through Murphy's findings that Law had formulated much of what was to be the Mississippi System prior to his being granted the charter for the General Bank in May 1716. Murphy, as

---

[13]Ibid., pp. 1118–19.
[14]Ibid., p. 1120.
[15]Law was not referring to metallic specie, but to the new type of "credit."
[16]Ibid., p. 1121.

shown in table 4, helps to outline how Law used the framework of the Bank of England, the East India Company, and the South Sea Company to formulate the Mississippi System.[17]

TABLE 4

BANK OF ENGLAND		EAST INDIA & SOUTH SEA COMPANIES	
Assets	Liabilities	Assets	Liabilities
Specie Reserves Gov't Securities Loans to Private Sector	Shares Banknotes/deposits	Fixed/Working Capital Gov't Securities Colonial Trading Privileges	Shares

ROYAL BANK [BANQUE ROYALE] (EARLIER GENERAL BANK)		COMPANY OF THE INDIES [COMPAGNIE DES INDES] (EARLIER COMPANY OF THE WEST)	
Assets	Liabilities	Assets	Liabilities
Specie Reserves Gov't Securities Loans to Private Sector	Shares Banknotes/deposits	Fixed/Working Capital Colonial Trading Privileges	Shares

MISSISSIPPI COMPANY	
Assets	Liabilities
Specie Reserves Fixed/Working Capital Gov't Securities Loans to Private Sector Colonial Trading Privileges	Shares Banknotes/deposits

[17]Ibid., p. 1123.

This combined company served to realize three of Law's aims: the expansion of the supply of money, with shares serving as money as well as banknotes and deposits; management of France's debt; and the development of the real economy. Law's "success" with his Mississippi System led not only to the Mississippi Bubble, but influenced the South Sea Company in England, and thus aided in the creation of the South Sea Bubble.[18]

---

[18]Ibid., pp. 1122–23.

The Mississippi Bubble 6

John Law began General Bank in May of 1716, a time when France was economically devastated. The late seventeenth century and early eighteenth century had been especially cruel to the French people. Under the reign of Louis XIV, France had fought wars almost continuously from 1689 to 1713, first with the League of Augsburg and then against Great Britain, Austria, Holland, and parts of Spain in the War of the Spanish Succession. In addition to the loss of life and financial costs of these wars, the French suffered through famines in 1693 and 1694, the loss of manpower and skilled labor resulting from the persecution of the Huguenots, and the extraordinarily cold winter of 1708–1709.

The War of the Spanish Succession (1701–1713) was fought mainly on foreign soil, which weighed heavily on the government treasury as it financed armies fighting in various theaters throughout Europe simultaneously. This financing was provided by floating debt, known as *billets de monnaie*. These certificates were first issued in 1701 to the owners of old coin and bullion who were delivering their specie for recoinage. But because the Paris mint was so far behind in striking and delivering new coins, this paper money was issued instead. The ever-increasing war needs led to overissue, with the expected depreciation in their value soon taking place. The *billets de monnaie* were made legal tender in Paris to stop this depreciation. Additionally, a royal proclamation was made on December 26,

1704, calling for 7½ percent interest to be paid on these notes. Legal tender status was extended to the provinces on April 12, 1707.

To finance the war, bills were issued on various royal agencies, adding to the *billets de monnaie* already in circulation. By 1708, the total supply of *billets de monnie* had reached 800 million *livre tournois (l.t.)*. This large increase in the supply of debt, on which the French government was obligated to pay interest, created a tremendous burden. To alleviate the financial strain, the Controller General of Finances, Nicolas Desmaretz, converted the 800 million *l.t*, in *billets de monnaie* into 250 million *l.t.* of *billets d'état*[1] and lowered the interest rate on the new notes to 4 percent. However, taxes could not be paid with these new notes, as was the case with *billets de monnaie*, despite both notes being payable by the government. This provision served to replace specie with these new paper notes.

During this period, the French working class continued to deal in hard-money because both types of *billets* were issued in denominations too large for wage payments. More importantly, the common man harbored a healthy distrust for government-issued paper money. In spite of the *billets'* legal tender status, Hamilton indicates that, "sellers accepted them for goods only at their market value in terms of specie, which varied from 20 to 50 percent of par."[2] These fluctuations in value made both types of *billets* unacceptable as mediums of exchange, and created a basic skepticism about paper money in general. It was this skepticism that prevented the establishment of a bank of issue.[3]

After the massive military buildup to wage war from the previous two decades, the French economy was to undergo a dramatic shift to peacetime operations. To resist the deflationary effects of this change in the economy, Desmaretz declared that money would

---

[1]Hamilton describes these financial instruments as equivalent to treasury bills.

[2]Earl J. Hamilton, "The Political Economy of France at the Time of John Law," *History of Political Economy* 1 (1969): 125.

[3]Ibid., pp. 123–26.

be gradually devalued by approximately 40 percent from December 1, 1713 to September 1, 1715. The initial effect on prices was mixed, with lower prices in Paris, and higher prices in the cities of Marseille, Toulouse, and Bordeaux in 1714. But by 1715, prices throughout France had plunged.[4]

Louis XIV died in September of 1715 with France's indebtedness being 3½ billion *livres*, or 159 *livres* per person. In spite of numerous taxes and rigorous tax collection, the state could not pay its debts. France was technically bankrupt and was forced to restructure its debt. This restructuring was accomplished by a combination of reduction, repudiation, and renegotiation.

Philip, Duke of Orléans, came to power after the death of Louis XIV. He ruled as Regent of France from 1715 to 1723 during the minority of Louis XV, who was the great grandson of Louis XIV. Philip replaced Controller-General Desmaretz with the Duke of Noailles, who was given the unenviable task of reducing the state's debts. All of the long-term debt owed by the government was refinanced, with city governments, particularly the *Hôtel de Ville* in Paris, acting as intermediaries. For a fixed return, investors would lend money to the municipalities, who in turn would lend the money to the state. Tax revenues would then be assigned to the municipalities to pay the interest due the bondholders. The state was the big winner in these transactions, at the expense of bondholders. The state's floating rate debt was then subject to a *Visa*[5], which reduced the floating debt from 597 million *livres* to 198 million *livres*. This new debt was in *billets d'état*, of which the government issued 250 million *livres*, 198 million *livres* toward the old debt, and 52 million *livres* for its own account.

How the various types of old, floating-rate debt was changed into *billets d'état* depended, in theory, upon the type of debt that

---

[4] Earl J. Hamilton, "Prices And Wages At Paris Under John Law's System," *Quarterly Journal of Economics* 51 (November 1936): 51; "Prices And Wages in Southern France Under John Law's System," *Economic History Supplement to the Economic Journal* 3, no. 12 (February 1937): 444.

[5] Agency in charge of cancellation or repudiation of debt.

was converted, whether the owner of that debt was the original purchaser, or whether the debt was paid for in cash. However, there was speculation that the size of the bribe to the Pâris Brothers, who operated the *Visa*, was the overriding factor in how much of a particular person's debt was replaced with the *billets*.

In addition to the financial destruction imposed by the *Visa*, Noailles established the "Chamber of Justice" in March of 1716. Murphy describes the Chamber of Justice as follows:

> The Chamber of Justice was an extraordinary commission established to judge and punish financiers and profiteers deemed to have made their wealth in a dishonest manner at the expense of the Crown. It was not a new phenomenon—there had been four Chambers of Justice in the seventeenth century in 1601, 1607, 1625, and 1661. They fulfilled a dual role, providing a blood-letting . . . and at the same time holding out hope of raising badly needed revenue for the Crown. Under the 1716–17 Chamber of Justice 8,000 people were investigated with just over half, 4,410, taxed a total of 220 million *livres*. In some less fortunate cases people found guilty were sent to the galleys, imprisoned, or locked in stocks and pilloried. Unlike some of the earlier Chambers of Justice, no one was executed.[6]

As was the case with the *Visa*, the Chamber of Justice was not true to its name in doling out tax levies. It was rife with corruption, and the wealthy financiers were treated favorably at the expense of a less fortunate, less wealthy class, who shouldered the brunt of the financial punishment. This inequities created a rebellion against the Chamber, which directly affected the collection of these taxes. Only 95 million *livres* were actually collected of the 220 million levied, with the majority being paid in depreciated paper. Noailles is said to have estimated the effective amount raised through the Chamber as only 51 million *livres*.

Like all other odious tax schemes, the Chamber of Justice, combined with the *Visa*, stifled the French economy. The wealthy were

---

[6]Antoin Murphy, *Richard Cantillon: Entrepreneur and Economist* (Oxford: Clarendon Press, 1986), pp. 56–57.

not inclined to spend or invest, credit tightened, and bankruptcies increased. Recognizing the damage inflicted by the Chamber, Noailles had it discontinued in March 1717.[7]

John Law obtained an exclusive charter (20-year term) for the General Bank in May 1716, and soon the Bank began operations in his home. Law picked the board of directors, the officers, and its first employees. Hamilton speculates that "no other national bank in history—not excepting the Reichsbank under Hjalmair Schacht or the Bank of England under Montagu Norman—has ever been so completely dominated by a single man."[8] The Bank's protector was none other than Law's old friend, the Duke of Orléans.

In the beginning, banknotes were to be payable in specie of the weight and standard of the date. The Bank was not subject to taxation, nor were foreigners' deposits subject to confiscation, in the case of war. Depositors would receive banknotes on sight for their coin. The Bank could open deposit accounts, which could be withdrawn, or through which an amount could be transferred to another party, similar to today's check writing. Bills and letters of exchange could be discounted by the Bank. However, the bank was not to engage in trade, maritime insurance, or commission business. There was no limit placed on the number of banknotes that could be issued by the bank. It was left to John Law's judgment as to the amount of banknotes to be in circulation.[9]

On May 20, 1716, the organization of General Bank was revealed. The Bank's capital totaled 6 million *livres*, comprised of 1,200 shares at 5,000 *livres* each. Murphy points out however, that:

> The effective capital base of the bank was much smaller than this due to the fact that only one quarter of the capital was to be subscribed in specie money and three-quarters

---

[7]Ibid., pp. 54–57.

[8]Hamilton, "The Political Economy of France at the Time of John Law," p. 145.

[9]Andrew McFarland Davis, "An Historical Study of Law's System I & II," *Quarterly Journal of Economics* 1 (April, July 1887): 298–99.

in *billets d'état* (a type of government security). The *billets d'état* were then at a discount of about 60 percent so that the effective amount of capital to be subscribed was:

Specie	1.5 million
Billets d'état (4.5 x 0.4)	1.8 million
	3.3 million *livres tournois*

Thus, at most, the effective capital base of the Bank would have amounted to 3.3 million *livres*, but even then capital was to be subscribed in four equal installments. It is believed that only one installment was actually paid up so that the General Bank started its operations with 825,000 *livres* (£52,700).[10]

A tremendous amount of government debt remained outstanding in spite of the amount lopped off by the *Visa* of 1716. It's estimated that, in addition to the abundant amount of long-term debt outstanding in the form of annuities, some 250 million *l.t.* was outstanding in the form of *billets d'état*, along with 215 million *l.t.* more in other obligations of the state. With this tremendous amount of debt and only an undercapitalized bank to work with, John Law needed another vehicle to lower interest rates. This vehicle was the Company of the West, which originated in the summer of 1717.

The idea for the Company of the West came from Le Gendre d'Arminy, who was the brother-in-law of financier Crozat. Crozat owed a large tax liability from the *Visa*, and wished to submit his ownership of the Louisiana trade lease as payment for this tax. Law made a grand proposal for the Company and was given permission to sell shares in the company in August of 1717. The company issued 200,000 shares at 500 *l.t.* each, or a total capitalization of 100 million *l.t.* These shares could only be purchased with *billets d'état*, which at the time where discounted between 68 and 72 percent. Thus, the effective capitalization was more like 30 million *l.t.* in

---

[10]Murphy, *Richard Cantillon*, pp. 70–71.

total, or 150 *l.t.* per share. The Company of the West's principal asset was the exclusive trading privilege with Louisiana that was granted by the French government. The privilege was received in exchange for the company's conversion of the government's debt into company stock at a lower interest rate.[11]

Initially, General Bank was prudently operated by Law and his staff. The banknotes issued by the bank were fully backed by specie. During the Bank's first 31 months, the supply of money in France was increased only 3 percent by the Bank's notes. The Bank met every obligation on demand and instilled a great deal of confidence for itself with the French public. By this time the operations of the Bank had expanded outside of Paris into the provinces. Law persuaded the Regent to order receivers to accept and redeem banknotes, and further, to remit tax receipts to Paris only in notes. Thus, circulation of the notes became widespread at a much quicker rate than would have taken place without such coercion.[12] It was Law's view that the power of the state should be used, if necessary, to force the use of banknotes, and that these notes should not bear interest, but be payable at site. He felt that the payment of interest on these notes created distrust amongst the people.

On April 10, 1717, it was decreed that all taxes and revenues of the State be paid in banknotes and received at par for that purpose. It is this date that is recognized as the first intervention of the state on behalf of General Bank, although as mentioned above, the provinces had received orders from the State six months prior to this. The provinces were united in their opposition to the use of the banknotes, and the Duke of Noailles was forced to follow up with supplementary decrees no less than three additional times, issued September 12, 1717, February 26, 1718, and June 1, 1718, before the opposition finally succumbed.[13] On December 4, 1718, General

---

[11]Ibid., pp. 71–73.

[12]Hamilton, "The Political Economy of France at the Time of John Law," p. 145.

[13]Davis, "An Historical Study of Law's System," pp. 303–05.

Bank formally became the Royal Bank, although the outstanding stock of the bank had already been purchased by the government prior to this date.[14]

The share price of the Company of the West in May of 1719 was still languishing, selling at a discount to their nominal issue price of 500 *livres* per share. For Law to fully set in motion his system, buying momentum was needed to spur an increase in the share price. His first move was to merge the Company of East Indies and the China Company together with the Company of the West. The new company was known as the Company of the Indies (a.k.a. Mississippi Company). To accomplish this alliance required funds, to pay off the heavy debt of both the China and East Indies companies, to outfit existing ships, and to build new ships. The Company could then exploit the colonial trade that was now under its complete control. The Mississippi Company then took over the Company of Africa on June 4th, which required further funding. To generate the needed capital, Law proposed issuing 50,000 shares at 500 *livres* per share, with a premium of 50 *livres* per share due immediately. Parliament refused to approve the issue, but the Regent stepped in and unilaterally granted approval by a decree of council on June 17th. By this time, the price of the shares had risen to 650 *livres*, undoubtedly buoyed by the issue of 159.9 million *livres* in banknotes by the Royal Bank in five installments, the first in January 1719 for 18 million, 20 million more in February, two infusions in April totaling 71.9 million, and 50 million more in June.

Activity in Mississippi Company shares began to pick up, with Law fueling the fire by allowing the new issue of 50 million shares to be purchased in 20 monthly installments of 25 *livres* each. Law did not want interest in the old shares to wane while promoting the new shares, thus, in modern parlance, he created a rights issue, whereby only owners of old shares, called *mères*, could purchase new shares, called *filles*. For every four old shares owned, an investor could buy one new share Murphy explains:

---

[14]Hamilton, "The Political Economy of France at the Time of John Law," p. 145.

These rights could be sold once they had paid the premium and the initial installment (50 *livres* plus 25 *livres*). Indeed, a decree of 27 July suggests that it was only necessary to pay the 50 *livres* premium and that the first payment of subscriptions was deferred till 1 September. In this way he maintained interest in the *mères*, thereby ensuring that holders such as the Regent and his followers made significant capital gains, but also provided a cheap way for others to come into the market by buying *filles* through monthly installments, when existing holders of old shares decided to realize some of their capital gains by selling their partly paid *filles*. But, above all, Law through the issue of partly paid shares provided leverage for investors to make capital gains that were a multiple of their initial investment. For example, if shares rose to 1,000 then the holder of a partly paid *fille*, assuming he had just paid the 50 *livres* premium, could make a profit of 450 *livres* (1,000−50+(25x20) by selling his *fille*, a profit nine times his initial investment.[15]

This new marketing ploy, allied with the expanded money supply, helped to increase investor interest in the shares of the Company of the Indies and the share price went over 1,000 in the middle of July.

On July 20, 1719, the Company of the Indies was awarded the profits of the Mint for a nine year period. The price to acquire these profits was 50 million *livres*, payable over a fifteen-month period. Within a week of this latest acquisition, the Royal Bank was allowed to increase the issue of banknotes by 240 million *livres*, and on July 25th, 220,660,000 *livres* worth of notes were issued. To enhance the value of the company's shares, Law then declared a dividend of 12 percent (60 *livres*) payable in two half yearly payments in 1720. The very next day after declaring the dividend, Law floated a new rights issue hoping to raise the 50 million *livres* needed to pay for the Mint purchase. As put succinctly by Murphy:

> Law had moved extremely quickly. He had increased the money supply and so oiled the speculative wheels of the

---

[15]Murphy, *Richard Cantillon*, pp. 77–78.

stock market, he promised an extremely high dividend to increase the attractiveness of shares, and he was channelling more shares on to the market.[16]

This time Law priced the shares at 1,000 *livres* each, with the company of course gaining a 500 *livre* premium on each share. To buy these new shares, called petites *filles*, the purchaser had to own 4 *mères* and 1 *fille*. The petites *filles* were to be paid in twenty monthly installments of 50 *livres* each. To create a sense of urgency, Law only gave investors 20 days to subscribe to these rights. This stoking of the speculative fire was not needed, for the share price had moved over 1,000 *livres*. Murphy draws upon four sources to construct the following table of Mississippi Company share prices for a three week period in late July and early August, 1719.

25 July	1,300	(Piossens)
29 July	1,500	(Piossens)
11 August	2,250	(Dutot)
9 August	2,330	(Giraudeau)
4 August	2,940	(Giraudeau)[17]

The rise in the share price continued, reaching 5,000 *livres* in September. With the public interest in buying the shares at a fever pitch, Law turned to refinancing more of the government debt. Once again Law floated Mississippi Company shares, in an attempt to lend the King 1.2 billion *livres* at a 3 percent interest rate. This new financing was to refinance France's remaining *billets d'état* in addition to replacing all of the state's *rentes*, or long-term obligations.

Law made four share issues in the fall of 1719 that totaled 324,000 shares: 200,000 were issued in late September, with

---

[16]Ibid., p. 78.

[17]Piossens, *Mémoires de la régence de S.A.R. le Duc d'Orléans Durant la minorité de Louis XV roide France* (1729), p. ii.; Dutot, *Réflextions politiques sur les finances et le commerce* (1738); Giraudeau, *Bibliothèque de l'Arsenal* (Paris), MS 4061. This manuscript is also to be found in the Bibliothèque Mazarine (MS 2820) and the BN (MS 14092); cited in ibid.

124,000 more issued a week later on October 2nd and 4th. The share price was 5,000 *livres*, with payment for the shares to be made in ten monthly installments of 500 *livres*. These new shares came to be known as *cinq-cents*.

These new issues were to raise 1.5 billion *livres*, an amount 14 times greater than the total of Law's first three stock issues combined. Law had struck while the fire was hot. But only a fraction of this amount was raised, because investors who purchased *cinq-cents* only put up 500 *livres* to acquire their rights, the rest to be paid in nine installments. In fact, if investors were having trouble making the monthly payments, Law would adjust the payment schedule to call for quarterly payments. Law was a master at developing ways to market the shares of the Company to the general public. In addition to the small down payment feature, Law developed an option market for the shares, called *primes*, in 1720. The Royal Bank made low interest loans for share purchases, and the shares were made bearer securities, thus providing anonymity of ownership. This later feature was important, given the people's memories of the 1716 *Visa* tax.

But the principal fuel that drove the market was the continuous increase in newly created banknotes, supplied by the Royal Bank. By the end of 1719, the total amount of banknotes had increased to one billion *livres*, and Law, through his tool, the Royal Bank, was far from finished. In May of 1720, banknotes were to total 2.1 billion *livres*.[18]

Near the end of 1719, share prices had risen to 10,000 *livres*, and more than a few investors wanted to sell their shares and realize their profits in specie. At this point, the Regent stepped in with various decrees to repress the attempted realizations. On December 9th, the company was granted the monopoly for the refining and separation of precious metals. On December 21st, banknotes were fixed at a 5 percent premium over silver coin. Silver could then only be used for payments under 10 *livres*, with gold to be used only for

---

[18]Ibid., pp. 130–31.

payments less than 300 *livres*. In addition, all foreign letters of exchange could only be paid in notes. "Law foresaw that, unless he could prevent the circulation of coin, it would all be quietly remitted across the border."[19]

On December 30, 1719, the company set the dividend for 1720 at 40 percent on the par value of 500 *livres*. Given a market price of 10,000 *livres*, the dividend amounted to a 2 percent yield, or a 4 percent yield on the recently issued *cinq-cents*. The company's income could not have paid that dividend from current income. Thus, it is not viewed as legitimate, but yet another of Law's tools to hype the stock price. Still, this dividend was only half the income the holders of *rentes* had received from the French government, prior to being forced to relinquish *rentes* for shares in the company. In fact, many *rentes holders* resisted the redemption. However, Law, upon being named Controller-General of France in January 1720, issued an ultimatum that *rentes* not redeemed by July 1st would be arbitrarily converted into 2 percent *rentes*.

As the share price began to wane, Law became determined to sustain the system by force if necessary. In late 1719, old gold and silver coins were confiscated. On January 20, 1720, a decree was passed authorizing the search of all homes for concealed coins. Eight days later it was decreed that banknotes were currency throughout the kingdom. The company was then allowed to search all buildings, with any specie seized benefiting the informer. Davis quotes from *Mémoires Secrets sur les Règnes de Louis XIV. et de Louis XV*:

> They excited, encouraged, paid informers. Valets betrayed their masters. Citizen spied upon citizen. This made my Lord Stair say that there could be no doubt of Law's Catholicity, since he established the Inquisition, after having already proved transubstantiation by changing paper to money.[20]

---

[19]Davis, "An Historical Study," p. 434.
[20]Ibid., p. 439.

Those who still dared to hold on to coin lived in constant fear, and Law did not stop there. On February 4th, it was announced that the wearing of any type of precious stone was to be prohibited after the first of March, the penalty being confiscation and a hefty, 10,000 *livre* fine. Two days later, the Royal Bank was allowed to issue 200 million *livres* in banknotes, and on the 9th all legal proceedings involving banknotes, which might arise, were to be brought before the Council. On the 11th, all "futures" transactions between individuals were banned, with the company being reserved exclusive right to sell "futures." On February 18th, it was decreed that goldsmiths were forbidden to manufacture or sell vessels of gold or silver, except for some articles of which the weight would be specified by the Regent. The next day, on February 19th, it was declared that no person was to have more than 500 *livres* in coin in his possession, and nobody, except goldsmiths and jewelers, was to have any articles of gold or silver. It was also announced that all payments of 100 *livres* and greater were to be made in banknotes, and all creditors of the State were ordered to be paid immediately.

Royal Bank was absorbed by Company of the Indies on February 22nd. John Law had the printing presses working full time to keep up with his ambitious banknote issue. Still the printers and clerks could not keep up. Engraved notes were abandoned, and more clerks were designated to sign the notes. In the case of 10 *livre* notes, so many had been created that many were issued without signature. These lax procedures created mistrust on the part of the public. To regain the appearance of conservatism, it was decreed that no more notes would be issued, except by decree at a meeting of the shareholders of the company.[21]

At the same meeting, in which it was decreed that the Royal Bank would be merged with the Mississippi Company, a number of other important measures were instituted. The King ceded to the company his 100,000 shares in the company, and in return he was credited with a 300,000 *livre* deposit at Royal Bank and the Company also committed to pay him 5 million *livres* a month for ten

---

[21]Ibid., pp. 436–41.

years. The total compensation was 900 million *livres*, or 9,000 *livres* per share. This was close to the then market price of 9,545 *livres* on February 22nd. The share price had peaked on January 8th at 10,100 *livres*. Thus Law was able to cash out the King very close to the market top.

At this same meeting, Law announced the closing of the Company's office for the purchase and sale of shares. Prior to its closure, this office had supported the share price of the Company at a high level. Murphy explains the purpose of the office:

> Ostensibly this was to bring some order to the market and prevent transactors being duped by some of the "sharks" who frequented the rue Quincampoix where the shares were traded. In reality it was to provide official support for the share price to prevent it falling below a certain minimum floor price. This policy had monetized the Mississippi shares and greatly expanded the liquidity of the economy.[22]

These measures combined to produce a precipitous decline in the price of the company's shares. Within a week, the price fell from 9,545 *livres* to 7,825 *livres*, a 26 percent decline. Law had anticipated that there would be a movement out of shares and banknotes into specie, and had prepared for this event with his decrees of early February. On February 25, Law announced an augmentation of specie, raising the *louis-d´or* from 25 to 30 *livres* and other coins *pari passu*. Murphy speculates that:

> This augmentation was meant to signal to the market that a diminution of specie was imminent, The message to specie holders was clear—move out of specie and into banknotes as specie would be worth less in terms of the money of account once the diminution was announced.[23]

Two days later Law repeated the decree that prohibited a person from holding more than 500 *livres* in coin.[24] Thus the Bank

---

[22]Murphy, *Richard Cantillon*, p. 132.

[23]Ibid., pp. 137.

[24]Davis, "An Historical Study," p. 440.

could then refuse to convert more than 500 *livres* for any one person, and have the law to point to. Law had thus given people two choices as to what form their wealth could be in, banknotes or shares.

On March 5th, Law announced several policies. The first was to reopen the office that bought and sold the company's shares. This office was now known as *bureau de conversions*, and was buying Mississippi Company shares at a guaranteed price of 9,000 *livres*. This measure served to again monetize the company's shares. Davis explains:

> With a fixed price attached to them, they became at once a part of the circulating medium, if not of the kingdom, at least of Paris. They were not receivable in payment of taxes, they were not made a legal tender, but they were convertible at will at a fixed price into bank-notes which fulfilled those purposes. Dutot calls attention to that phase of this decree. He says they—the shares—"became proper to fulfil the uses of money."[25]

Next another augmentation of the coin was announced. *Louis-d'or* went from 36 *livres* to 48 *livres*, and the *ecu* was raised from 6 to 8 *livres*. This augmentation foreshadowed an impending diminution of specie against banknotes at the Bank. It was also ordered that all bank loans would be called at maturity. As Davis indicates: "This order was peremptory, and the inference is unavoidable that the bank had no other business than loans on margins."[26]

Within a week, on March 11th, a series of diminutions was decreed. These diminutions were intended to demonetize specie. Gold was to be demonetized by May 1st, with the silver marc to be demonetized in monthly diminutions from 80 *livres* to 30 *livres*, by December 1720. It is clear that Law's intent was to have only two circulating mediums in France, banknotes and Mississippi Company shares, both of which were under his control.[27]

---

[25]Ibid., p. 444.

[26]Ibid., p. 443.

[27]Murphy, *Richard Cantillon*, p. 138.

The decrees of March 5, 1720 have been viewed differently by various writers. Davis summarizes these views:

> According to Daire, it was the keystone of the system, and fully realized Law's economic thought. It transformed the bank into a reservoir of the circulating medium, which the paper of the Company of the Indies would keep at any height, since it served both as feeder and outlet. Should money become too abundant, it would find its way to the bank for conversion into shares. Should the reverse be the case, shares would be converted into notes. Dutot says the decree was a mortal blow to the system. Law was confronted with the necessity of sustaining either notes or shares, but was unable to protect both. Shares at the time represented more than fourfold the value of the notes, and he chose the shares. In taking this step, Dutot thinks a mistake was made. Law was responsible for the notes; but Dutot does not think him responsible for the speculation, intimates that the regent must be held responsible for the decree, and says that it was counselled by enemies of the system. Forbonnais says the decree absolutely decided the fall of the system. He thinks the purpose was to sustain the promised dividend by absorbing into the treasury shares on which the dividend would then not have to be paid, and that Law was attached to the principle of the multiplication of wealth, and believed that the shares would assume the property of money in circulation. Louis Blanc denounces the decree as a crime, which has unjustly been imputed to Law, and believes it was issued in the interest of the Court. The decree announcing that no more shares would be bought and sold saved the system by ruining several great lords. The decree of March 5 saved several great lords by ruining the system.[28]

However, the decree of March 5th was not the last "shoe to drop." That distinction could possibly be assigned to the decree of May 21st, which Murphy describes as "the Beginning of the End." In table 5 Murphy outlines the phased price reductions of shares and banknotes set forth in the decree of May 21st:

---

[28]Davis, "An Historical Study," pp. 445–46.

TABLE 5

	SHARES	BANKNOTES	REDUCTIONS IN SILVER 11 MARCH DECREE
Prior to decree	9,000	10,000 . . . 100	80
21 May	8,000	8,000 . . . 80	65 (1 May)
1 July	7,500	7,500 . . . 75	55
1 August	7,000	7,000 . . . 70	50
1 September	6,500	6,500 . . . 65	45
1 October	6,000	6,000 . . . 60	40
1 November	5,500	5,500 . . . 55	35
1 December	5,000	5,000 . . . 50	30

Source: Antoin Murphy, *Richard Cantillon: Entrepreneur and Economist* (Oxford: Clarendon Press, 1986), p. 148.

By this decree, Law was acknowledging that his decree of March 5th, guaranteeing the 9,000 *livre* price of the shares and at the same time stipulating that silver's value would be diminished in phases, could not be sustained. Murphy explains in a footnote that:

> Law argued that as silver was to be reduced from 80 to 30 it was illogical to hold that shares and banknotes should not be reduced also. . . . In retrospective comments on the System he argued that he wanted to make such reductions in March but had been prevented from doing so by vested interest groupings.[29]

This comment adds credence to Louis Blanc's view that the system was sacrificed for the benefit of political insiders. As quoted by Murphy, Law admitted to the public:

> It was necessary to fix a just proportion betwixt the bank bills and the specie, therefore we were forced to deviate from

---

[29]Murphy, *Richard Cantillon*, p. 156.

the former proportion, without which, the actions and bank bills must unavoidably have lost their credit.[30]

As much as Law had hoped to drive specie out of circulation, by the use of both market incentives and heavy handed coercion, the French public could not be completely persuaded of Law's view that paper money was better than gold and silver. The decrees of March, 1720 had but slight success in attracting specie to the Royal Bank. By May 21st, with the public holding 2.1 billion *livres* in banknotes and another 600 million *livres* at the bank or about to printed, the Royal Bank's specie holdings amounted to only 21 million *livres* in silver and 28 million in gold.

For the investing public, Law's decree of the 21st cast a cloud of doubt over what was supposed to be an infallible system. Now all of a sudden, shares were subject to diminution similar to specie. The public outcry forced Law's friend, the Regent, to demote Law and place him under house arrest. The once revered Law, along with his system, was now despised, and on May 27th, the Regent attempted to stem the negative tide by revoking the May 21st decree. Two days later, he announced further an augmentation of specie along with rescinding the prohibition on the holding of gold and silver.

In spite of the system now being in shambles, Law was reappointed to a lesser position within the government, *Intendant Général du Commerce*, and was reaffirmed as director of the Royal Bank. Law attempted to keep the system afloat through the end of 1720, but the public did not fall for any more of Law's financial razzle-dazzle. In table 6 Murphy shows the downward trend in Mississippi Company share prices from June through November of 1720.

Although share prices declined, they did so gradually, which is a departure from other bubbles, where asset prices typically break sharply. Murphy explains:

---

[30]John Law, *The Present State of the French Finances* (London, 1720), p. 105; Quoted in ibid., p. 149.

TABLE 6

	High	Low
June	6,350	4,517
July	5,403	4,450
August	4,724	4,367
September	5,133	4,167
October	5,167	3,200
November	3,967	3,300

Source: Antoin Murphy, *Richard Cantillon: Entrepreneur and Economist* (Oxford: Clarendon Press, 1986), p. 151.

However, there is an explanation for the gradual collapse in the price of Mississippi shares, a phenomenon not mirrored by the collapse of the South Sea scheme where the fall in the price of shares was sharper and more sudden. In France large quantities of specie had been withdrawn from circulation, through Law's measures and hoarding on the part of the more perspicacious public. Most wealth holders in France faced the classic Keynesian two-asset choice, that is money (banknotes) or bonds (shares of the Mississippi Company). The price of shares did not collapse because French investors were locked in to holding either shares or banknotes. At times the price of shares rose because investors felt marginally more confident about them than about holding banknotes.[31]

The way to truly gauge the affects of the excessive money creation by Law is to look at the French exchange rate, which sank from 20 pence sterling in May to 6 pence in September, and was so low it was not quoted for the last three months of 1720. It was the *livres* plunge against the pound sterling that is the manifestation of the bursting of the Mississippi Bubble. In table 7 Murphy juxtaposes this exchange rate relationship with Mississippi share prices in both *livres* and sterling for selected months in 1720.

---

[31]Ibid., p. 152.

TABLE 7

	January	March	May	July	September
Mississippi share prices (*livres*)	9,085	9,000	9,018	4,895	4,367
Exchange rate pound sterling/*livres*	30.0	32.3	39.3	50.7	92.3
Mississippi share price in sterling (1/2)	£302	£279	£229	£97	£47

Source: Antoin Murphy, *Richard Cantillon: Entrepreneur and Economist* (Oxford: Clarendon Press, 1986), p. 152.

While the drama of this boom and subsequent bust was being played out, what was the effect upon the lives of the French working class? As is the case with all government created monetary schemes that expand the supply of money, money is not spread equally over the populace; certain groups gain access to the money, i.e., government, borrowers, and speculators, while other groups, such as, the working class, elderly, and savers are excluded.

Hamilton has developed index numbers to represent commodity prices, money wages, and real wages in Paris during the period of John Law's system.[32] The commodity price index is a composite of food, raw materials, wholesale building materials, and household staples. However, articles with "sticky" prices, such as bread and salt, were omitted. The money wage index is comprised of only daily wages of skilled and common labor, and excludes salaries. It is Hamilton's intention that, "the present index numbers presumably do not underestimate the rise of prices and wages during the Mississippi Bubble."

To gain a sense of the effects imposed upon the French populace from the tremendous increase in the supply of money, we shall

---

[32] Hamilton, "Prices And Wages At Paris Under John Law's System," pp. 50–54.

juxtapose these indexes at selected months in the Mississippi Bubble story.

TABLE 8

	May 1716	Dec. 1718	July 1719	Jan. 1720	May 1720	Sept. 1720	Dec. 1720
Commodity Prices	100.7	112.1	116.1	171.1	189.7	203.7	164.2
Money Wages	102.7	102.7	125.8	125.8	141.2	161.9	118.1
Real Wages	101.4	89.4	113.7	74.4	75.3	84.8	82.5

The selection of the above dates was not random, each date is significant:

May 1716 ⟶	General Bank is chartered
Dec. 1718 ⟶	General Bank becomes Royal Bank
July 1719 ⟶	Royal Bank expands banknote issue by 221m
Jan. 1720 ⟶	Company share price peaks at 10,100
Mar. 1720 ⟶	Law's diminution of silver
May 1720 ⟶	Law's diminution of banknotes and shares
Sep. 1720 ⟶	Paris price index peaks
Dec. 1720 ⟶	Law's system falls apart

The above indexes illustrates the disparity between prices and wages. As prices continued to spiral upward, wages, although increasing a certain sporadic intervals, never kept pace with prices. Included in the above price index are building materials, which experienced the largest percentage increase of any of the goods included in Hamilton's index for the year 1720. As is the case with many modern increases in the supply of money, construction activity in Paris was growing at a frantic pace, doubling the cost of building materials. The following year, after the bubble's collapse, three-quarters of this gain was lost.[33]

---

[33]Ibid., pp. 65–66.

The boom and bust was not confined to Paris. Hamilton has compiled wage and price indices for three cities in southern France during the Mississippi Bubble period: Marseille, Toulouse, and Bordeaux.[34] Hamilton summarizes his findings:

> From June to October 1720 prices advanced 36 percent, at Bordeaux, 47.2 percent, at Toulouse, and 12.3 percent, at Marseille . . .
>
> At their highest points, in October, prices at Bordeaux were twice as high, and at Toulouse 2.4 times as high, as the respective averages in 1716–1717. Owing to the catastrophic pestilence that ravaged Provence in the late spring and summer of 1720, the peak at Marseille, reached in September, was 2.7 times as high as in the base period. In their apogee, in September, commodity prices at Paris stood only 2.04 times as high as in 1716–17.[35]

Concerning wages, unfortunately, an acceptable wage series could not be found for Bordeaux, but Hamilton was able to secure financial records for Marseille delineating wages for seven different classes of labor, and wages for four different grades of labor in Toulouse. Wage rates in both cities fluctuated moderately between the years 1711 through 1718. As Law's system began to take shape in earnest, in 1719, wages moved up sharply in the second quarter, but still lagged behind prices. As the system collapsed in the fourth quarter of 1720, real wages at Toulouse stood at 82.2, and 87.8 at Marseille, reflecting the same phenomenon as that in Paris. Wage increases were always a step behind commodity price increases. In the systems aftermath, wage-earners continued to be decimated in Toulouse, as the real wage index sank to 76.3 in the third quarter of 1721. This did not occur at Marseille, due to the plague's decimation of the population, thus making labor scarce. Real wages began to rise in 1721 and continued through 1725.[36]

---

[34]Hamilton, "Prices And Wages In Southern France Under John Law's System," pp. 441–61.
[35]Ibid., pp. 455–56.
[36]Ibid., p. 459.

By all measures, John Law's money machine was to spell disaster for the French working class, whether they lived in Paris or in the provinces. As Hamilton states, "Law's System was a catastrophe to the labouring class."[37]

As we recount the story of John Law's Mississippi System and its eventual collapse, it is clear that Law was a man very much ahead of his time. He created a bank which in many ways could be considered the prototype of modern central banks. Through the vehicle of the Royal Bank, Law created paper money out of thin air and tried in vain to escape the confining clutches of gold and silver specie, a struggle that has been taken up by subsequent inflation mechanics from Benjamin Strong and Montagu Norman to Alan Greenspan. The following quote from Law sums up his view:

> An abundance of money which would lower the interest rate to 2% would, in reducing the financing costs of the debts and public offices etc. relieve the King. It would lighten the burden of the indebted noble landowners. This latter group would be enriched because agricultural goods would be sold at higher prices. It would enrich traders who would then be able to borrow at a lower interest rate and give employment to the people.[38]

Law's theories were virtually a blueprint for Keynesian economics, as Murphy says, "Keynes can be termed as post-Lawian!"[39]

Salerno quotes Rist's critical summary of Law's ideas:

> Law's writings . . . already contain all the ideas which constitute the equipment of currency cranks—fluctuations in the value of the precious metals as an obstacle to their use as a standard . . . the ease with which they can be replaced by paper money, money defined simply as an instrument of circulation (its function of serving as a store of value being ignored), and the conclusion drawn from this definition

---

[37]"Ibid., p. 461.

[38]John Law, *Euvres complètes*, P. Harsin, ed. (Paris, 1934); reprint Vaduz, 1980), II, p. 307; 'Mémoire sur les banques' (translation); quoted in Murphy, *Richard Cantillon*, p. 129.

[39]Murphy, *Richard Cantillon*, p. 129.

that any object can be used for such an instrument, the hoarding of money as an offence on the part of the citizens, the right of the government to take legal action against such an offence, and to take charge of the money reserves of individuals as they do of the main roads, the costliness of the precious metals compared with the cheapness of paper money.[40]

Given modern central bankers and their respective governments' willingness, if not eagerness, to reach for the easy-money tonic to revive an ailing economy, it is no surprise that an overindebted Britain turned to John Law's medicine in 1720. The manifestation of Britain's financial chicanery is known as the South Sea Bubble, which had its origins with the founding of the Bank of England in 1694, an institution that Law sought to emulate with his Royal Bank.

---

[40]Charles Rist, *History of Monetary and Credit Theory: From John Law to the Present Day* (New York: Augustus M. Kelley Publishers, [1940] 1966), p. 65; quoted in Salerno, "Two Traditions in Modern Monetary Theory: John Law And A.R.J. Turgot," *Journal et des Etudes Economistes* 2, no. 2/3 (191): 15.

The South Sea Bubble 7

Late seventeenth-century England was a time of increased trade, industrial expansion, and, of course, war. All of these elements created the need, at least in the minds of the British, for a public bank. England's close relations with Holland during this period gave the British a first-hand view of the vast Dutch economy and the important linchpin for that economy, the Bank of Amsterdam. In fact, after the founding of the Bank of Amsterdam in 1609, other public banks began to be formed: local banks at Rotterdam, Delft, and Middelburg, the Bank of Hamburg in 1619, and the Bank of Sweden in 1656. English merchants began to be exposed to public banks throughout Europe, and thus various proposals began to surface for a public bank in England.

But it was the British government that had the greatest need for a public bank. William of Orange, when he came to the throne in 1689, hoped to gain popularity by abolishing the hearth tax.[1] But, needing money to fight the war against France, in addition to the civil war in Ireland and Scotland, William imposed a series of other taxes: the poll tax, stamp tax, window tax, land tax, and taxes on peddlers, hackney coaches, births, bachelors, marriages, and burials.

---

[1]The hearth tax was a tax on all dwellings except cottages, and was levied based upon the number of hearths or stoves that were in a given dwelling. The tax was very unpopular and as can easily be imagined, hard to collect.

As is inevitable, government revenue was not increased in the same proportion as the increase in the tax levies. Even had all the taxes been collected, the war expenses were far in excess of the highest revenue potential of the taxes.[2]

Parliament made provisions allowing tallies to be issued on future sources of government tax revenue. At first these orders were issued against the proceeds of specific taxes. But the government then began to issue against revenue in general. These tallies were made assignable and eventually the majority of this government debt was held by England's goldsmith-bankers.

In December of 1671, Charles II was in need of funding to finance his Navy. He called upon the bankers for help, but they refused. After a debate in Council, the King decided to prohibit certain payments out of the Exchequer. His proclamation of January 5, 1672 has come to be known as the "Stop of the Exchequer." The Stop allowed the King to pay whom he wanted, with others being out of luck. Keith Horsefield quotes two items in the proclamation that allowed for the King's payment discretion: "all other public services and support of the government" as well as "all other payments appointed by Warrant under the Privy Seal or Royal Sign-Manual."[3] The second item enabled the King to direct payments even on stopped funds. Not surprisingly, payments continued to flow to areas of the government. The most serious losses were absorbed by the goldsmith-bankers. With the government not making payments on their tallies, bankers were in turn forced to stop payment. Although Charles told the bankers to make payment to their customers, the banks did not have the money to do so.

The Stop was originally to only last for one year, but was continued until January 1674. But by that time the damage had been done, as Horsefield indicates: "By then the funds on which the

---

[2]Andreas M. Andréadès, *History of the Bank of England 1640–1903* (New York: Augustus M. Kelley, [1909] 1966), pp. 55–56.

[3]Keith J. Horsefield, "The 'Stop of the Exchequer' Revisited," *The Economic History Review* 15, no. 4 (November 1982): 513.

orders had been drawn were all expended, so in practice the Stop became permanent."[4] The immediate effect of the Stop was that credit quickly evaporated. The goldsmith's notes became worthless, and subsequently many goldsmith-banks folded. The long-reaching effect of the Stop was the postponement of joint-stock banking for ten to fifteen years.[5]

After the Stop, the King had difficulty borrowing money. Thus, the British government needed a bank, and of the many schemes proposed, the one advanced by William Paterson had the most promise. Paterson is described by John Giuseppi as, "one of those men whose ideas range some years ahead of their time and who have a streak of the true visionary about them, but never quite reaches genius."[6] Paterson and the spokesman for his financial backers, Michael Godfrey, took their plan for a "Bank of England" to Charles Montague, a Lord of the Treasury who subsequently, in 1694, became Chancellor of the Exchequer. Paterson's financial backers were all men of great substance, influential politically and all Protestants.

In spite of such backing, the plan was vigorously debated upon reaching parliament for approval. The Tories feared that the Bank's operation would greatly strengthen the Whig government, while the goldsmiths and money lenders feared being demolished. Also, some merchants worried that the Bank would pose a threat to their trade business, and there were even some Whig supporters who feared that the Bank of England would make the monarchy financially independent of the Parliament. Prior to the proposal reaching Parliament, there were concerns within the government about the scheme, most prominently, the note issue. Paterson and his promoters recognized the tremendous profit potential from note issue, by expanding on what goldsmiths were enjoying on a local basis. The

---

[4]Ibid., p. 514.
[5]Ibid., pp. 511–28.
[6]John Giuseppi, *The Bank of England: A History from its Foundation in 1694* (Chicago: Henry Regency, 1966), p. 9.

government took a dim view of the bank encroaching on its domain—the manufacture and control of England's currency.

Paterson's first proposal was denied by Parliament because, as Clapham says: "It looks as though they thought the proposal was for the issue of legal tender bank notes; and apparently that is what it was."[7] Paterson quickly formulated a second proposal, which made no mention of bills, except in clause 28 of the Act, which was added to the original draft in a separate schedule. Sir John Clapham makes the comment that "the clause looks like an afterthought."[8] This proposal was brought before the Cabinet by Montague, who submitted that £1,200,000 be raised, which in turn would be lent to the government at 8 percent, under the condition that the subscribers be incorporated and that £4,000 a year go toward their management expenses.

Paterson's scheme was debated at length by the Cabinet. Finally, it was agreed that a bill containing the proposal should be put before Parliament, where it was passed after being adroitly attached to an ordinary finance bill. The act was not known as the Bank of England Act, but as:

> An Act for granting to their Majesties several Rates and Duties upon Tunnage of Ships and Vessels, and upon Beer, Ale and other Liquors: for securing certain Recompenses and Advantages, in the said Act mentioned, to such persons as shall voluntarily advance the Sum of £1,500,000 towards carrying on the War against France.[9]

Thus, the Bank in its early years was called the "Tunnage Bank." On April 25, 1694, the Act received the Royal Assent, and subscriptions for £1,200,000 of the £1,500,000[10] began to be taken. Opponents of the Bank attempted to postpone the commission, but

---

[7] Sir John Clapham, *The Bank of England: A History*, vol. I: 1694–1797 (London: Cambridge at the University Press, 1966), p. 16.

[8] Ibid., p. 17.

[9] Ibid.

[10] The £300,000 difference was to be raised by annuities.

Queen Mary squelched the antagonists immediately. King William, plain and simple, needed the money to fight France. The subscription books were opened at "Mercer's Chappell" on June 21st, with £300,000 being subscribed the first day. The entire £1,200,000 was completed by July 2nd. The first subscribers were the King and Queen for £10,000,[11] followed by 1,267 individual holders. Subscribers were required to pay 25 percent of their subscribed amount in cash.[12]

As remarkable as the speed of filling the subscription is how quickly the subscription's full sum made its way into the Exchequer. The Bank had promised to complete the operation by January 1, 1695, but full funding was in fact completed by mid-December. Clapham indicates that "this had been done while its capital, nominally of the same amount, was still only 60 percent paid up; and even some of this £720,000 existed in the form of subscribers bonds which, rather sanguinely, were 'reckoned as cash'."[13]

The Bank aggressively sought deposits from its very beginning, devising three "methods in keeping running cash." These methods are described by Clapham:

> ... by "Notes payable to Bearer, to be endorsed", by "Books or Sheets of Paper, wherein their Account to be entered", or by "Notes to persons to be accomptable". The third method is a kind of deposit receipt, as is shown by an August decision that only "acomptable notes" be given for foreign or inland bills of exchange until "the mony be actually received". The second method anticipated the modern passbook: it blended with the third under a rule by which people who drew notes (cheques) should have receipts for their deposits "and ye particulars of the Bills drawn are to be entered on ye side". It is the first method which produced those bearer notes "without which the Bank could hardly

---

[11]£10,000 was the maximum subscription allowable. Ten other contributors besides the King and Queen contributed the maximum amount.

[12]Giuseppi, *The Bank of England*, pp. 11–12.

[13]Clapham, *The Bank of England*, p. 20.

have carried on business"; and the third from which the cheque developed, for the holder of an "acceptable note" could create "drawn notes" against it, for himself or others.[14]

The Bank of England's note issue monopoly was only limited by the formal order that prohibited it from issuing notes in amounts exceeding its capital. However, as early as 1696, critics of the Bank complained of the free use of notes. Clapham quotes from a broadsheet issued in connection with the recoinage of 1695–96 entitled *The Mint and Exchequer United*:

> the Bank was limited by Act of Parliament not to give out Bills under the Common Seal for above £1,200,000; and if they did every Proprietor was to be obliged . . . to make it good, so that they give out Bank Bills with interest for but £1,200,000. But they give the Cashier's notes [observe the term he uses] for all sums (*ad infinitum*) which neither charge the Fund nor the Proprietors, which seems to be a Credit beyond the intention of the Act . . . and never practiced before by any Corporation, and almost a Fraud on the Subject.[15]

In spite of frequent attacks, the Bank prospered. Its promoters were all influential Whigs, which ensured the support of both the government and the commercial world, both of which would run to the Bank's aid whenever it was threatened. This success was reflected in the price of the Bank's stock which hit the unprecedented price of £108 in January, 1696. But two dangers loomed on the horizon: the recoinage and the Land Bank project.

England's coinage was depreciating daily as a result of continual clipping and other debasement, e.g., iron and copper coins being silvered over. The situation was so severe that trade was at a standstill, attracting the attention of Parliament, which passed the Re-Coinage Act of 1696. This act forbade the exchange, sale, or receipt of any coins, clipped or unclipped, gold or silver, for more than their

---

[14]Ibid., p. 21.

[15]Ibid., p. 22.

nominal value. Additionally, the law called for a £500 fine for anyone caught in possession of coin clippings, plus the offender would be branded on the right cheek with a capital R. And, if this was not enough, only professional goldsmiths were allowed to buy or sell bullion. Any house suspected of containing bullion could be inspected at any time. If bullion was found on the premises, the owner was required to prove that the bullion was not the product of clippings or melted coin. County sheriffs were required to pay £40 to anyone who procured the conviction of a clipper. The law went even further to provide incentives to snitch on a person's bullion holding neighbor. Any "clipper" who was able to secure the guilt of two other "clippers" would receive a pardon, and the ambitious apprentice who informed on his master was made a freeman of the City. This "war on clipping" which ultimately led to the harshest of penalties, execution, inspired the clergy to protest. Two difficulties that the Exchequer was forced to grapple with concerning the Re-Coinage Act were the expense of the recoinage and more importantly, the decision as to whether the coins should keep their old standard or be issued at a lower one.

The expense of the operation totaled £2,703,164 and was covered with difficulty. This ultimate cost was far in excess of that estimated in the beginning. The Bank also was naïve about the consequences of the recoinage, as Andréadès writes:

> Possibly too, if the Bank had realized the difficulties it would have to face—the depreciation of its stock and notes, the suspension of payments and of dividends—its directors, in spite of their courage and intelligence, would have refused to enter upon such a formidable adventure, more especially since they were already threatened by the Land Bank.[16]

The question of whether the new coins should keep their old standard or be issued at a lower one was to be debated vigorously. William Lowndes, the Secretary of the Treasury, developed the idea

---

[16]Andréadès, *History of the Bank of England 1640–1903*, p. 99.

that lowering the standard of fineness of the coins while continuing to call the coins by their former names, would defray the expense of the recoinage. Lowndes's report was met with a crushing rebuttal from John Locke, who is quoted by Andréadès:

> But this, however ordered, alters not one jot the value of the ounce of silver, in respect to other things, any more than it does its weight, this raising being but giving of names at pleasure to aliquot parts of any piece. No human power can raise the value of our money their double in respect of other commodities, and make that same piece or quantity of silver, under a double denomination, purchase double the quantity of pepper, wine, or lead, an instant after such proclamation, to what it would do an instant before.[17]

In spite of Lowndes's suggestion being the prevailing view, Montague's support, combined with Locke's keen analysis, led to passage of the resolution to preserve the old standard.[18]

The Land Bank proposal was put forth by Dr. Hugh Chamberlain and John Briscoe. Their idea was to raise a public loan twice that of the Bank of England. This loan would be backed by the security of landed property and have an interest rate of 3½ percent. Chamberlain and Briscoe fell into the same trap as John Law, viewing paper money backed by land as equivalent, if not superior, to gold or silver. Their plan called for the printing of money equal to the total value of all property. As Andréadès points out, these promoters knew that government coercion was needed to carry out their scheme:

> The promoters did not deny that the public preferred the precious metals, and that in consequence if the Land Bank were forced to pay in gold, it would soon have to suspend its

---

[17] This quote is taken from Locke's pamphlet entitled, *Further considerations concerning raising the value of money*. Andréadès indicates that this pamphlet has been reprinted at the end of McCulloch's *Principles of Political Economy*; quoted in Andréadès, *History of the Bank of England 1640–1903*, p. 101.

[18] Andréadès, *History of the Bank of England 1640–1903*, pp. 90–102.

payments. But they proposed to overcome this difficulty by making the notes inconvertible and legal tender.[19]

The British government in the spring of 1696 was again, as is the case with all governments, in need of money, and the Land Bank received Royal Assent on April 27th by way of a Ways and Means Bill. The bill was to raise £2,564,000, with the interest on the loan to be covered by a salt tax. But alas, the Land Bank act died as quickly as it was engendered. Only £7,100 was subscribed, with £5,000 of that being the King's investment. With the government on the brink of bankruptcy, the Exchequer stepped in with an issue of Exchequer bills to fill the breach. Also, the King was able to secure a loan from the Dutch in the amount of £500,000. This scrambling for funds was due to the fact that the government had borrowed all that the Bank of England could lend, based on it not being able to lend an amount more than its capital. The Bank's bills had fallen to a 10 percent discount. Additionally, its stock had dropped from £107 to £83 with the passage of the Land Bank proposal and the subsequent floating of the Exchequer bills. The Bank had many competitors, with all of them issuing their own paper. As Carswell writes:

> Neither recoinage nor expanding trade could have been financed without paper money, which was issued during the war in increasing quantity from the Exchequer, the Bank of England, and the innumerable goldsmiths and running cashes of Lombard Street.[20]

It was the damage that the Bank received from the Land Bank scheme, the recoinage, and its pesky competitors, that led its promoters to seek aid from the government in the form of monopoly status. The case was made that, for the Bank to be useful to the State, its notes must not be faced with competition which "causes distrust and contracts credit instead of enlarging it."[21]

---

[19]Ibid., pp. 104.

[20]John Carswell, *The South Sea Bubble* (London: The Cresset Press, 1960), p. 18.

[21]Andréadès, *History of the Bank of England 1640–1903*, pp. 107–10.

The main provisions of the act in 1697, which gave the Bank of England monopoly status, were:

(a) The Bank would add £1,001,171 to its capital,

(b) Subscriptions could be paid 80 percent in Exchequer bills, 20 percent in Bank notes,

(c) Subscribers were to be incorporated in the company,

(d) The Bank was granted monopoly status for the duration of its charter until August 1, 1711, since no other banking corporation was to be established by an Act of Parliament,

(e) 8 percent interest was guaranteed by the salt tax on tallies accepted in payment by the Bank,

(f) Before opening the subscription for the additional capital, the original capital was to be paid up to 100 percent for each proprietor,

(g) The Bank was authorized to issue notes to the amount of its original capital (£1,200,000), plus the sums to be subscribed, on the condition that they were payable on demand,

(h) All property of the Bank was exempt from taxation,

(i) It was to be a felony to forge or tamper with Bank notes.[22]

By consequence of this act, £200,000 in banknotes and £800,000 in tallies were drawn out of circulation, thus the discount on the remaining Bank notes disappeared, and these banknotes began to circulate without bearing interest.[23]

England's war with France also ended in September, 1697, relieving the government treasury of the burdensome expense of the war, perhaps just in time. Early in 1697, over £5 million of short-term government borrowings were due and had to be extended, and to add to the distress, the Malt Lottery loan subscription in April

---

[22]Ibid., pp. 111–12.
[23]Ibid.

was a complete flop.[24] The government's credit was repaired with the help of the Bank of England, three years of peace, and the successful floating of New East India Company stock in 1698, which in turn loaned £2 million to the Exchequer. This new entity, like the Bank of England, was allowed to use the government's debts that it owned as a "fund of credit."[25]

The tranquility of peace was not to last long, as the War of the Spanish Succession began when Louis XIV of France marched into the Spanish Netherlands in February 1701. William, who hated Louis XIV, was eager to join the European coalition. However, the public was not in the mood for more of William's war and commercial unrest. In spite of three years of peace, taxes and interest rates had remained high, hangovers from the previous war debts. But with a hostile enemy just across the English Channel, the English joined the fray in earnest, especially after the death of King William in 1702.

The long and bloody confrontation was to again tax England's treasury. The Bank of England supplied short-term funding, with long-term funding supplied mainly by the sale of 96 to 99 year annuities. Sidney Godolphin was named as Lord Treasurer in 1702 by Queen Anne, and was, in the view of Dickson to manage "the national finances with great care and skill."[26] Godolphin seemed to be able to raise funds to fight the French with relative ease, being aided by the British army's battlefield conquests, which bolstered investor confidence. The war's expense was running at between £8 million to £9 million per year. This unprecedented expense was far greater than what could be extracted from the populace by way of new taxation. Thus, tax revenues through the end of the century

---

[24]The Malt lottery was to issue 140,000 £10 tickets, raising £1,400,000. Only 1,763 tickets were sold, the rest of the tickets were used by the Exchequer as cash. P.G.M. Dickson, *The Financial Revolution in England: A Study in the Development of Public Credit 1688–1756* (New York: St. Martin's Press, 1967), p. 49.

[25]Ibid., p. 57.

[26]Ibid., p. 59.

were mortgaged with long-term debt. From 1704 through 1710, the British government's long-term borrowings totaled £10.4 million. In addition to these loans from the public, Godolphin borrowed £1.7 million in Exchequer bills from the Bank of England, and obtained loans from the East India Company.

By this time, the public had become anxious about the length of the war and its cost, both in blood and financially. The harsh winter of 1708–09, which led to a bad harvest the following summer, pushed up prices. This inflation and the failure of peace talks at The Hague in August was followed by a bloody battle at Malplaquet in September and created an adverse political climate that led to a new Tory Ministry the following year. The new Ministry sacked Godolphin on August 8, 1720, with Robert Harley being named Chancellor of the Exchequer two days later. In May of the following year Harley was named Lord Treasurer.[27]

In the meantime, Sir John Blunt and his partners had transformed the Sword Blade Company into a finance company in order, as Carswell says, to "annex for themselves as large a part as they could of the politico-financial empire that had been carved out by the Bank of England."[28] The Sword Blade Company's business was to acquire estates with the proceeds from stock issues that were paid for in government obligations. The obligations chosen were Army Debentures, issued by the Paymaster of the Forces. The market price of these debentures was £85, for which the holders were then offered Sword Blade stock valued at £100. The government was thus traded their own debt instrument, at a discount, for their land.

In the spring of 1704, the Bank of England took offense of the activities of the Sword Blade Company, serving notice to the Treasury that the monopoly clause of the Act of 1697 was being violated by Mr. Blunt and his company. Blunt contended that the Act of 1697 only prohibited rival corporations set up by an Act of Parliament, which the Sword Blade Company was not. By May of 1707, the Bank

---

[27]Ibid., pp. 59–64.
[28]Carswell, *The South Sea Bubble*, p. 34.

managed to get the Treasury's promise that it would take action against Sword Blade Company and to fortify the Bank's privileges.

The Sword Blade Company provided good, healthy competition for the Bank of England, but the Treasury needed money, and the Bank was willing to lend £1½ million at 4½ percent.[29] With the Treasury getting what it wanted, it in turn extended the Bank's charter to 1732, along with allowing the bank to double its existing capital of £2,201,171. The additional capital was raised before noon the same day subscriptions became available. Andréadès provides a breakdown of the Bank's capital position at this point:

Capital of the Bank	£2,201,171
This Capital doubled	£4,402.343
And increased by the £400,000 now advanced	£4,802,343
To which must be added for the Exchequer bills	£1,775,027
Total	£6,577,370[30]

The activities of the Bank, along with those of the Sword Blade Company and the East India Company, ensured that there was plenty of money available. As Carswell writes: "The war had encouraged, not checked, the advance of wealth and the multiplication of paper. It was no uncommon thing, now, for a man to have made a 'plum,' as current slang described £100,000."[31]

As was the case in the Bank's original charter, the Bank's note issue was only restricted by the amount of its capital. Andréadès quotes H.D. Macleod's stinging criticism of this scheme:

> Now, to a certain extent, this plan might be attended with no evil consequences, but it is perfectly clear that its principle is utterly vicious. There is nothing so wild or absurd in John Law's *Theory of Money* as this. His scheme of basing a paper currency upon land is sober sense compared to it. If

---

[29]Ibid., pp. 34–37.

[30]Andréadès, *History of the Bank of England 1640–1903*, p. 122.

[31]Carswell, *The South Sea Bubble*, p. 43.

for every debt the Government incurs an equal amount of money is to be created, why, here we have the philosopher's stone at once. What is the long sought Eldorado compared to this? Even there the gold required to be picked up and fashioned into coin.[32]

The new Chancellor of the Exchequer, Robert Harley, had inherited from his successor, Godolphin, a mountain of debt, and the immediate problem of having to satisfy the creditors of the Navy, all of whom were anxious to be paid. Harley received proposals from John Blunt and George Caswell of the Sword Blade Company, and from Sir Ambrose Crowley, a large contractor with the Navy Board. The Blunt-Caswell plan essentially called for the incorporation of the Navy and other creditors, along with cancelling the state's debt to them in exchange for stock.

Harley was not flush with options. He did not have the cash to pay the floating debt, and had no alternative to the Blunt-Caswell proposal. On June 12, 1711, the plan was given Royal Assent. The government's short term creditors, holding close to £9 million, were to be incorporated under the Great Seal as "the Governor and Company of Merchants of Great Britian Trading to the South Seas and other parts of America and for encouraging the Fishery."

This new entity, in exchange for extinguishing £9 million in government debt, was given a monopoly on trade with South America, on the east coast from the River Orinoco to Tierra del Fuego, and for the entire west coast. This region had for some time held an allure of riches to the British. Thus, it was the perfect vehicle to placate the government's creditors, given its potential for high profits. In fact the British, since the reign of Queen Elizabeth, had attempted to break the Spanish stronghold on the Americas, either by force or license. This attempt, like the others, was to fail. The opening of this market would come much later, in the nineteenth century, with the political independence of the Spanish colonies.

---

[32]Ibid., p. 124.

The establishment of the South Sea Company coincided with the British expedition in August, 1711 against Quebec, and the planning of an Anglo-Dutch attack on the Spanish West Indies. Dickson theorizes that: "It can therefore be regarded as part of a three-pronged drive for empire in the new world, though there is little doubt that in fact this grand design was three-quarters bluff, intended to assist Harley's peace negotiations."[33]

At war's end in 1713, the South Sea Company's trading rights were defined. The company had permission to send, annually, one 500 ton ship to trade at the fairs of Cartagena or Veracruz and to send 150 ton supply ships to supply food to the factories. In addition, it was given a thirty year contract to supply African slaves to New Spain. This contract called for the delivery of 4,800 slaves per year of a specified condition, with the company paying taxes on 4,000 of these. The King of Spain was to receive 10 percent of the company's slave trade profit in addition to the 28 percent of all other trading profits. This limited amount of trading privilege, along with the payment to the King of Spain of his share, left but a meager return for the company.

It was to take over two years to even come close to selling out the South Sea subscription. The books were finally closed on Christmas of 1713, with a total of £9,177,968 having been raised, an amount smaller than the £9,471,324 envisaged by the South Sea act. The company was to receive annually £550,678 in interest and £8,000 for management from the government. In the beginning the government paid promptly. But this situation changed, and by the summer of 1715 interest was six months in arrears. With no interest income coming in and little progress made in starting trade with Spanish America, the company was quickly in financial trouble. In 1712, 1713, and 1714 the proprietors were given the option of receiving dividends in cash or in bonds. In 1715, no choice was given, dividends were paid in bonds; and, in 1716, dividends were paid in the form of stock. Fortunately for the subscribers the stock was now at par.

---

[33] Dickson, *The Financial Revolution in England*, p. 66.

From 1712 through 1715, the government used South Sea stock to pay creditors and to secure loans. "For the use of the public," £2,371,402 of the company's capital had been set aside; plus £500,000 in stock was created for the government's use by the South Sea Act. This use of funds was not popular, and eventually, in 1717, the company was able to shed its encumbrances, with Parliament proclaiming that government deficiencies were to be paid, in the future, out of the General Fund. Also, by this date progress had been made on the trade front and the company appeared to have weathered its difficult beginnings.

By the use of the South Sea Company vehicle, the government was able to rid itself of its floating debt. However, this repayment did nothing to fund the burden of the war expense that had reached its height at that time (1711). To fund this shortfall, Harley created Exchequer bills on a massive scale to handle the short-term needs, and used the Bank of England as receiver for £9.2 million in lottery loans floated in 1711 and 1712 to cover the revenue deficit. Harley went on to float smaller lottery loans in 1713 and 1714, with the Bank acting as receiver. One loan was to discharge the debts of the Civil List, and the other was to go to the public service.[34]

The War of the Spanish Succession was finally over in 1713. England and the other participants had each created a huge mountain of debt with which they were forced to contend. On September 29, 1714, Britian's national debt stood at £40,357,011. Additionally, there were over £4½ million in Exchequer Bills outstanding, not to mention debts of back-pay to the army and foreign subsidies of unknown amounts. The government undertook a massive restructuring of its debts in hopes of lessening the interest burden.

This restructuring was accomplished through three conversion Acts. The first called for the conversion of the 1711–12 lottery loans outstanding and half of the 1705 Bankers' Annuities debt to be exchanged into 5 percent stock to be managed by the Bank of England. The second act reduced the interest rate on various debts

---

[34]Ibid., pp. 59–75.

owed to the South Sea Company and the Bank of England. The third act established a sinking fund for reduction of the national debt and called for reducing the interest rate on Exchequer bills to 1½ percent.

These measures, which were implemented between 1715–1719, were for the most part successful, reducing the government's annual interest charge by 13 percent and providing welcome relief to the state. Although the yield on government obligations had been lessened, most holders of the government stock felt their principal was more secure. This feeling was reflected in the market price of government stock. At the end of 1717, the stock was trading four points above its par value.

However, there was one finance problem left to be solved, that of the high and virtually perpetual interest to be paid to annuitants. These annuity holders would have to be persuaded to exchange their annuities for redeemable stock. The Treasury turned to the South Sea Company in 1719 with a plan for this conversion. The interest payable on these annuities was £135,000 yearly, thus the Treasury calculated that this interest should be capitalized at a market price of eleven and a half years purchase, or £1,552,500. To be added to this was £168,750 in back interest owed the company and the £778,750 the company was to lend to the Exchequer. Thus, the total increase in the state's debt was to be £2.5 million as a part of this conversion.

In the spring of 1719, it turned out that only two-thirds of the subscription was taken. As a result the South Sea Company's capital increased by £1,746,844 to a total of £11,746,844. The subscription, which was payable in fifths, was fully funded in December 1719, with the company receiving £592,800. The Exchequer was to be paid £544,142. This was raised by selling £520,000 in new stock at £114 in July. The company's claims against the state now stood at £193,582. Thus, when all was said and done, the company had made a tidy profit of £242,240 from the operation, and had £24,000 in stock still in hand. This success led to a much bigger operation of the same kind the following year.

Across the Channel, in 1719, John Law's system was at its height and was viewed with more than a twinge of jealousy and concern from the Brits. Law's debt conversion had already inspired John Blunt and his fellow Sword Blade partners. But what concerned the British government was the ever increasing flight of capital leaving London to seek the much-talked-about returns to be enjoyed in Paris. With further debt conversions being contemplated by the government, it did not want this loss of capital to hinder its plans. These fears were raised when rumors began to circulate that John Law was opening a large "bear" account to depress British Government stocks. At the same time, another rumor had him buying the East India and South Sea Companies so as to become the financial czar of Europe. But the government's worries were pointed in the wrong direction. John Law's system was about to fall apart, and besides, Law had a very ambitious imitator in Sir John Blunt, who was about to embark on his own grand scheme.

Two categories of debt were particularly troublesome to the government. One was the ninety-six and ninety-nine-year annuities which had been sold when interest rates were high, and could not be redeemed by a lump-sum payoff or a sinking fund (they could be redeemed only if annuitants were persuaded voluntarily). The other category was miscellaneous debts, which were being redeemed by Walpole's sinking fund at approximately £750,000 per year. Total government debt service, not including management charges and amounts converted into stocks already, was over £1.5 million per year, and as Carswell relates:

> this was the amount negotiators at the Treasury were concerned to disguise as a single huge redeemable annuity to the South Sea Company. For this purpose it was necessary to represent the whole as a capital sum. . . . To keep one's head in the maze of South Sea finance, it is important to lay firm hold on the fact that the capital figures were mere paper calculations.[35]

---

[35]Carswell, *The South Sea Bubble*, pp. 103–04.

The capitalization of the redeemable debt was straightforward and totaled approximately £16 million. As for the irredeemable annuities, the capitalization was much more difficult to formulate. The overriding objective was to reduce the cost of this debt as much as possible. This was accomplished by capitalizing these annuities at their original term of years, but without regard to the date they were issued. Ninety-nine and ninety-six year annuities were capped at 5 percent for twenty years, with the thirty-two year and the Lottery annuities being capped at 6 percent interest for fourteen years. The total capitalization for the annuities was £15 million, making the grand total £31 million.

Against this staggering sum of £31 million, an equal amount of South Sea stock was to materialize when debt holders would voluntarily exchange one for the other. The amount of stock that the company would issue for any given debt was to be decided by the market. Thus, as was the case with the 1719 conversion, the higher the price of the stock, the more profitable the conversion would be for the Company.

The Company's deal with the government in regards to the conversion was very precise: for every pound of yearly expense spared the government, the Company received a pound a year from the government. The exception to this was on irredeemables where the Company would receive only 14 shillings for each pound the government was saved. This was worth £40,000 a year to the Exchequer. The ultimate savings to the government was to come after seven years, when the government would only pay 4 percent on all of the converted debt, a savings of roughly £400,000. In addition this obligation could be redeemed. Thus, the government was allowed to pay off the debt in total whenever it might be able. It was calculated that if the interest savings were applied according to sinking fund principles, Britian's debt would be retired in twenty-five years. And if the prospect of being debt free was not enough incentive, the Company offered a carrot that was to be paid at the end of the one year conversion term: a gift to the Exchequer of £3 million, payable in four quarterly installments, to be used to pay off redeemable debts incurred before 1716, with any amounts that remained being available for use in whatever way the Exchequer desired.

This £3 million sweetener also served as an insurance policy for Blunt. If all of the redeemables were not converted, this £3 million would be available to pay these debts off. Thus, with the Bank of England owning most of these notes, the threat of repayment was enough for the Bank, which would not be able to reinvest the cash at attractive returns, to convert the debts it held for South Sea stock. Blunt knew that he would never earn, in the normal course of business, the £3 million in cash needed to make this promised gift, for every penny of income would have to go toward payment of the 5 percent dividend on the capital. What Blunt was counting on was a rise in the share price of South Sea stock to generate the needed funds.

Blunt calculated correctly that, if a boom in stock prices was engendered, holders of government annuities would quickly exchange this debt for the opportunity to make huge capital gains relatively quickly. The fuel needed for this boom was endogenous to the plan, as Carswell points out:

> The plan amounted to the injection into the economy which was already booming, of another £5 million or so of new money—ten times the injection of the previous year—with a simultaneous lowering of interest rates.[36]

The final days of 1719 brought news that spurred the fortunes of the South Sea Company. Peace between Spain and England had been declared on the terms of the latter, opening up trade passages to South America. The time had come for Blunt's grand plan to be presented to the Parliament. Chancellor of the Exchequer, John Aislabie, laid the plan before the House of Commons on the basis that the plan was forthcoming from the Company. Secretary Craggs followed with the suggestion that the House receive the plan. But to Aislabie's dismay, an influential Anglo-Irish Whig, Thomas Brodrick, suggested that the House consider other offers before it

---

[36]Ibid., p. 108.

accepted this one, and the measure was not voted on. This allowed the Bank of England time to make a rival proposal.

The Bank was suddenly put in a position of having to fight for the top financial perch upon which it had sat for so many years. For ten years the South Sea Company had slowly increased the amount of annual payments it received from the government, to over £500,000, and now the Bank was faced with the possibility that the South Sea Company would be the recipient of £2 million in annual annuity payments at its expense. It was feared that the loss of this conversion would relegate the Bank to being just an ordinary commercial bank, with its old enemy, the Sword Blade Company, the credit-creating agency behind the South Sea Company, depriving them of their lofty position within the London money market.

The bidding for the conversion was spirited. The critical deal point, which the Bank and the Company continued to make more and more attractive, was the amount to be given as a gift to the Exchequer. The South Sea Company's original £3 million was increased to £3½ million, only to be increased to £5½ million with the Bank's bid. But the Company finally won out by raising the stakes of the gift to £4 million certain to the Exchequer, with the possibility of as much as another £3½ million. The additional amount was dependent upon the amount of debt that was actually converted. Also, the Company promised to make the annuity open for redemption in four years rather than the seven years originally proposed, and, at the same time, reduce the interest rate to 4 percent. Finally, the Company offered to circulate £1 million in Exchequer bills with no management fee or interest. This was an offer that the Bank of England could not match, and the South Sea proposal passed in the House with ease. With the news of the Company's triumph, the traders in Exchange Alley bid the price of its stock up 31 points, from 129 to 160, and what a journalist of the time called "the English Mississippi" was underway.[37]

As the debt conversion was being negotiated and subsequently bid for, English pounds continued to flow across the channel into

---

[37]Ibid., pp. 98–113.

the awaiting tempest that John Law's system had now become. After hitting a high in January 1720, Mississippi Company shares had fallen. Law was now desperately trying to hold up the shares at the expense of his inflation ravaged currency, and the financial freedom of the French people. Law's proposals put forth in the spring, in hopes of salvaging the currency, were met with suspicion from the savviest of London's investors, who began to pull their money out of Paris and return it to the London market.

John Blunt and the rest of the South Sea stock promoters, like John Law in the case of the Mississippi shares, sparked the fire of speculation in the Company's shares by allowing the governing class the opportunity to be in on the ground floor of the stock issue. This virtually assured them a profit. Nearly all of London's bourgeoisie had purchased their shares prior to the publishing of the Bill calling for the debt conversion on March 17th. Subsequently, between March 19th and 21st, the share price soared from £218 to £320 on reports from Paris that John Law was taking criticism from the Regent and having nightmares. A second reading of the Bill on the 21st inspired a debate on the 23rd over whether the terms of the conversion should be fixed in advance and be written into the statute. The debate lasted six hours, with contrary news causing the price of the shares to trade in a broad range of 110 points, between £270 and £380. The company prevailed, which propelled the stock to £400 for a brief period before it retreated back to £330.

On March 25th, the Bank of England was further humiliated. It was announced that the entire debt held by the Bank (£3.75 million) that was not to be redeemed by the South Sea Company would be repaid by the end of the year. The payoff of this debt meant that the Bank would no longer be a national institution. Any support the Bank had enjoyed from those individuals in government that was now firmly behind the South Sea Company, with more than a few having been given shares in the company to enjoy in the speculation and reap the financial reward. The Bill finally received Royal Assent on April 7th. The Company had provided £574,500 worth of stock in bribes to government officials to get the bill passed, and now London was poised for the boom. Carswell added up the liabilities that the Company would incur over the next year (£11.4 million), which the profits of the conversion would have to cover.[38] A share price of £140 was needed to break even. On April 7th the stock stood at £335.

The South Sea Company's subscription and debt conversion was begun in April, with the Company's primary motive being very clear: to market its new stock while the share price was rising, while deferring the second conversion of government debt until August, when its share price was at its height (£1,000). This would maximize its exchange advantage over government debt holders. The Company's first stock subscription was on April 14th, with 2,250,000 issued at a per share price of £300. The terms of payment were 20 percent down, with the balance to be paid for over sixteen months with calls every two months.

The second issue came two weeks later, on April 29th, with 1½ million shares issued at a price of £400. The terms quickly became more liberal, 10 percent down, with the balance over twenty months payable in nine calls at three to four month intervals. With the market frantically trading up the stock, the Company made its third and largest issue on June 17th, issuing 5 million at £1,000 per share. Terms again called for 10 percent down, but payments were stretched over fifty-four months, with nine payments made semi-annually. The fourth, and final issue was made on the 24th of August, with 1,250,000 issued at, again, a £1,000 share price. The terms of this issue called for 20 percent down, with the balance to be paid over the next thirty-six months. Had all payment calls been made, the Company would have received £75,250,000 over the subsequent four and one-half years! The market had two vehicles with which to trade the South Sea Company: the actual shares and the subscription receipts.

Demand for the shares was enormous, as exhibited both by the increase in price and how quickly the shares were snapped up during the four offerings. The first was said to have been filled in an hour, the second and third issues in a few hours, and the final issue in

---

[38]Ibid., p. 127.

three hours. There was even talk of an additional issue, however it was scuttled in early September when the market was beginning to crumble.

The decision by John Blunt and the rest of the South Sea directors to begin with stock issues or "Money Subscriptions" as they were known, rather than the conversion of the government debt was driven by the following motives, outlined by Dickson:

> first, to the knowledge that they could legally increase their capital without any limit, provided they applied part of the proceeds to paying off the government's creditors; second, to their wish to take the exchanges in stages, rather than spoiling the market by taking them all at once. A third motive was, of course, their wish to cash as quickly as possible the cheque which the Government had handed them without waiting to see if there were the funds to meet it.[39]

When the Company began to convert the annuities to South Sea stock, the holders of these annuities were eager to get hold of the new South Sea shares and sell them in the now booming market, but the Company was not keen on a flood of shares pouring into the market, putting a damper on the share price. Annuitants or their attorneys showed up at South Sea House, with their title documents in tow, to sign their names and the annual amounts they received into the books. These documents were headed by an introductory statement that most of them, unfortunately, neglected to read. This preamble gave three South Sea clerks the power to subscribe the capital stock in whatever way the company saw fit to the annuitants. Rather than delivering shares, a book entry was made, with the actual stock not being delivered until December 30, 1720. This method was repeated in July and again for the third and, as it turned out, final debt conversion in August. The government creditors had thus exchanged their debts for no more than the expectation of possessing South Sea stock.

---

[39]Dickson, *The Financial Revolution in England*, p. 129.

The primary holders of the government debts were, not the unsophisticated masses, but no less than the powerful Bank of England, Million Bank, and a host of wealthy, powerful individuals. Dickson gives the result of their collective gullibility:

> 80% of the long and short annuities (the Irredeemables) and 85% of Government ordinary stock (the Redeemables) were converted into South Sea stock. The company's nominal capital increased by over £26m., on which the Government was to pay interest partly at 5% and partly at 4% until midsummer 1727, then entirely at 4%. Despite bitter pressure on the part of the disappointed public creditors in the winter of 1720–1, the exchanges were not rescinded, . . .
>
> When it put the accounts together, the company found that, thanks to the rise in the market price of its stock, it had been able to persuade holders of £26m. of the £31m. subscribable debts to exchange them for South Sea stock so over-valued that they only obtained £8.5m. of it.[40]

By the late spring, early summer of 1720, foreign buying began to push the price of South Sea stock ever higher, as investors fled Paris in ever increasing numbers. Also, specie from Holland began to arrive in London to be used for the purchase of shares. At the same time, the Company gave Exchange Alley a liquidity injection by giving the directors the power to lend money on the security of South Sea stock. This action produced £11 million in loans. At the same time, the Bank of England was throwing gasoline on the fire in the form of loans on its own stock. The government also got into the act by lending the South Sea Company £1 million in Exchequer bills that were subsequently used to purchase the Company's shares. Even the Royal African Company, which lent £102,000, joined the party.

The South Sea share price was now rocketing upward. At the start of June, the price was £600, and by the end of that month it stood near £1,000. This tremendous speculation led to a flood of other proposals for new companies in Exchange Alley. Many of the

---

[40] Ibid., pp. 134, 136.

proposed operations were swindles, with promoters marketing a particular stock with the tool of low down payments and deferred-payment plans, only to confiscate the down payments and leave the city. Some, however, were respectable ventures. The number of "bubble company" proposals hit its height in June, with 88 being promoted in that month. Only eleven more were sponsored the entire rest of the year.

Speculation was not limited just to South Sea shares or these "bubble companies." Other securities rose as well, along with the price of land, as the following quote of Lord Bristol, who was negotiating with William Astell over the price of a land parcel from Dickson, illustrates: "land has almost doubly increased in value since ye time I first fix'd for your final answer."[41]

Ironically, at the height of speculation in June, the pin that would eventually pop the bubble was being fashioned by the British government. On June 11th, the King's assent was given to the Bubble Act, which made it an offense to "presume to act" as a corporate body or to divert an existing charter to unauthorized ends. In August, four companies were found to be in violation of the Act: the English Copper Company, the Royal Lustering Company, the York Buildings Company, and the Welsh Copper Company. Although the Act had been enacted to keep capital from being channeled away from the South Sea Company, the writs against the four companies signaled the beginning of the steep fall in the price of South Sea shares. In spite of desperate attempts to increase the demand for shares by declaring a 30 percent Christmas dividend (*à la* John Law), a torrent of sell orders descended upon Exchange Alley. By mid-September the share price had dropped to £520, and by October the price was £200, on the its way to £120 in December. The bubble had exploded.[42]

---

[41]Letter Books of John Hervey, first Earl of Bristol (Wells, 1894), II, p. 126; Bristol to Astell August 4, 1720; quoted in Dickson, *The Financial Revolution in England*, p. 147.

[42]Dickson, *The Financial Revolution in England*, pp. 122–53.

After the "house of cards" had finally been leveled, the financial prospects of the South Sea Company were put in a clearer light. The Company's only asset, besides trading privileges that were for the most part unexploitable, was a stream of income from the Exchequer in the amount of £2 million per year. The bad news was that expenses for the coming year were £14.5 million. The South Sea Company was hopelessly insolvent.[43]

In spite of the Company technically being bankrupt, it was able to stay in business for many years through a massive reorganization engineered by Sir Robert Walpole. Walpole's ability to sift through the wreckage and decide who the winners and who the losers would be from this financial train wreck made him a revered and beloved man of such high reputation that he went on to rule England as Prime Minister for twenty years. This reverence for Walpole is evidenced by Clough's comment:

> He [Walpole] was able, moreover, to save for government bondholders about 60 percent of their investment, and he was successful in salvaging enough of the South Sea Company to keep the organization in business, eventually, however, with government securities as its only assets.[44]

Clough fails to realize that government securities were the only asset the company ever had. Furthermore, we can only wonder if the government bondholders at the time thought that taking a 40 percent "haircut" on their investment was a good deal.

Far from being an isolated mania engendered only by the urges of a populace with the gambling spirit, the South Sea Bubble was the inevitable result of a government living beyond its means. Britain had the help of some enterprising entrepreneurs who, with the example of John Law, produced the various schemes and institutions through which to create the money needed to pay for its wars and largess. As is always the case when paper money is created

---

[43]Carswell, *The South Sea Bubble*, pp. 238–39.

[44]Shepard B. Clough, *European Economic History: The Economic Development of Western Civilization* (New York: McGraw-Hill, 1968), p. 217.

illegitimately, some groups benefited at the expense of others, with speculation taking the place of honest work and production as the way to achieve wealth. This environment of frenzied speculation led to political corruption, great disparities of wealth, fraud, and violence. As aptly put by Andréadès:

> But all these must not lead us to infer that the South Sea crisis was beneficial to England. It had produced enormous agitation and an unjust redistribution of wealth and had very nearly ruined the Hanoverian monarchy. . . . Those who shared in it knew perfectly well that it was only a fraud, but hoped notwithstanding to make some profit out of it. . . . These speculators—and this is one of the most painful features of the crisis—represented all classes of society, and things were so arranged that the poorest man might ruin himself as easily as the millionaire.[45]

The big winner in this story of financial debauchery was, of course, the British government, which was able to transform an insurmountable mountain of debt, through their agent, the South Sea Company, and at the expense of the public creditors, into a much more manageable expense. In effect, a portion of the government's debt service was repudiated, with the financial pain being thrust upon those people who were least able to shoulder it, an unsuspecting public.

The South Sea bubble episode was relatively short compared with that of the Mississippi Bubble. The difference between the two bubbles was that Law used the Royal Bank to print more money, and thus sustained the system for a longer period of time. Conversely, the Bank of England stood apart from the South Sea government debt conversion. As the bubble burst, the Bank of England, concerned about its own survival, discontinued discounting, called in loans made against its own stock and loans made to the East India Company, and sold customers interest-bearing notes in an attempt to raise cash.[46]

---

[45]Andréadès, *History of the Bank of England 1640–1903*, pp. 143–44.
[46]Giuseppi, *The Bank of England*, p. 44.

If the Bank of England had been successful in outbidding the South Sea Company for the conversion of the government debt, a replay of the Mississippi bubble is a distinct possibility, the likely result being a British populace suffering even greater financial pain.

Increases in the Supply of Money, Speculative Bubbles, and the Austrian Malinvestment Theory 8

As we seek explanations for the causes of speculative bubbles, the forthcoming responses from the different strains of modern mainstream economic thought are far from satisfying. The Rational Expectations School, after much muddling of figures and formulas, comes to the conclusion that bubbles are not possible since all market participants act rationally and can foretell the future. As this volume has shown, speculative bubbles do occur, and market participants—people—cannot foretell the future, and do not necessarily act rationally. Econometrics has again struck out in its attempts to explain, let alone predict, the behavior of humans. But, of course, rather than admit that their tools are inadequate, the rational expectations group concludes that, empirically, it cannot be shown that speculative bubbles exist. Thus, they do not. This otiose view flies in the face of historical fact.

John Maynard Keynes, whose school of thought when followed as policy is the modern catalyst for speculative bubbles, wrote at length concerning speculation. Keynes recognized full well the damage that speculation and malinvestment could inflict on people. What Keynes did not recognize was the root cause of these episodes. Instead, he focused on the results which he thought were the causes. The following paragraph from Keynes sums up his view of speculation:

> there is the instability due to the characteristic of human nature that a large proportion of our positive activities depend on spontaneous optimism rather than on a mathematical expectation, whether moral or hedonistic or economic. Most, probably, of our decisions to do something positive, . . . can only be taken as a result of animal spirits.[1]

Keynes held the view, as reflected in the above quote, that these "animal spirits" lead to damaging speculation, and he, of course, prescribed government restrictions on investment to solve the problem.

So, on one end of the spectrum, we have the rational expectation camp, which says that all people—market participants—are rational, and, being in possession of all available data, can foretell the future. One hundred eighty degrees opposite the rational expectations group is Keynes, who saw all people as being possessed by "animal spirits," i.e., being irrational, which will thus cause frequent instability and speculation in an economy, with the obvious cure being intervention by the State, which is assumed to be rational.

By reflecting back on what has been written in here, it is obvious that speculative bubbles can and do occur. And if Keynes's "animal spirits" were the cause of speculative bubbles, these bubbles would have happened continually, *ad infinitum*, throughout history. Given the fact that this "animal spirit" is an inherent human trait that is not turned off and on, these speculative episodes would be constantly engendered through no other impetus but human nature. This is clearly not the case.

The three speculative bubble episodes just explored, besides having the obvious similarity that they all occurred, share the common trait that a government-sanctioned bank, along with government policy, created large increases in the supply of money in each economy, prior to and during these episodes. Each episode was in its own way different, especially the Tulipmania. However, the results were the same: boom, speculation, crash, and then financial pain.

---

[1]John Maynard Keynes, *The General Theory of Employment, Interest, and Money* (New York: Harcourt, Brace & World, 1964), p. 161.

Another common element to all three experiences was a man named John Law. Law was born in 1671, after the Tulipmania bubble, but he studied the workings of the Bank of Amsterdam, which played a part in the Tulipmania, greatly admiring its operation and its positive effect on the Dutch economy. The Bank of Amsterdam was the linchpin of the strongest economy in the world because of the soundness of its operation and therefore the Dutch currency. The Bank accepted coin and bullion and issued bank money against these deposits. All bank money was backed 100 percent (in the Bank's beginning) by specie and thus great confidence in this money was engendered.

Because of the soundness of this money and the Dutch free coinage policy, immense amounts of coin and bullion flowed to Amsterdam from other parts of Europe, America, and Japan. This torrent of coin and bullion is reflected in the deposits of the Bank of Amsterdam, which increased an estimated 60 percent in the five year period (1633–1638) which encompasses the Tulipmania episode. Total mint output of the South Netherlands for the 1636–38 period was two and a half times greater than the amount minted from 1630–32. This huge influx of money, albeit sound money, led, as Del Mar writes, to "the curious mania of buying tulips at prices often exceeding that of the ground on which they were grown."[2] The culmination of Tulipmania came in January 1637 when, for example, the price of the Witte Croonen tulip bulb rose approximately 26 times in the space of that month, only to crash to a price of one-twentieth of its peak price the first week in February of that same year.

After studying the operations of the Bank of Amsterdam during the course of his travels throughout Europe, Law began to formulate monetary theories and banking proposals, which in turn he

---

[2]Alexander Del Mar, *History of Monetary Systems: A Record of Actual Experiments in Money Made by Various States of the Ancient and Modern World, as Drawn From Their Statutes, Customs, Treaties, Mining Regulations, Jurisprudence, History, Archeology, Coins Nummulary Systems, and Other Sources of Information* (New York: Augustus M. Kelley, [1895] 1969), p. 351.

advanced to States throughout Europe. Law believed that silver and gold were ill-suited to serve as money, that their values were subject to fluctuation depending upon supply. Initially, Law's plan called for paper money that was backed by land, thinking that this paper money would better satisfy the qualities necessary in money.

Law was initially unsuccessful in selling his proposal to any European governments, even that of his native Scotland. His views also began to change, as he studied other banks including the Bank of England, which was formed in 1694. Law was impressed with the Bank of England's ability to pay for England's war against France with paper money. He began to view stocks as money and that they were superior to silver, thinking that they were inflation proof.

Law was finally able to find a taker for his scheme in 1716, when he began the General Bank in Paris. France at that time was devastated economically, after fighting the War of the Spanish Succession and piling up huge debts. Law was intent on refinancing this government debt so as to lower interest rates and stimulate the languid French economy. To accomplish this, Law began the Company of the West, whose only asset to speak of was the trading privilege with Louisiana. After selling shares to capitalize the company, Law refinanced the government's depreciated debt.

Law then set out to put his system in motion. He was finally able to convince the Regent to make the General Bank part of the State, with it becoming the Royal Bank in late 1718. Law then merged three companies together to form what has been commonly known as the Mississippi Company. With the Royal Bank issuing 159.9 million *livres* in fresh banknotes, the price of the Mississippi Company shares began to take off in early 1719. In the second half of that same year, with Royal Bank issuing another 220.6 million *livres* worth of banknotes, combined with Law's low down payment, and the extended terms method of marketing the stock, the price continued to climb, allowing Law to issue more shares. He then used the capital to refinance more of the government's debt.

The share price peaked at 10,100 *livres* in January 1720, aided by increases in the supply of money that was to total 2.1 billion *livres* by May of 1720. In the spring of 1720, the system was beginning to unravel, leading Law to issue a series of decrees attempting first to devalue silver, then to devalue shares and banknotes. With investors attempting to sell shares and convert the proceeds to specie, Law frantically tried to keep the system afloat, and in fact was able to do so, given the lack of specie due to hoarding and Law's policies. But by the end of the year, the bubble had been deflated. In September, shares were 43 percent of the high. Indeed, in pound sterling terms, Mississippi shares were only 14 percent of their highs, which more truly reflects the consequences of the massive increase in the supply of money engineered by Law.

While speculation was running rampant, commodity prices were exploding over the course of four years, not only in Paris, but in other cities in France. Some cities experienced worse inflation, and for some it was not as severe. The big loser was, of course, the laboring class, whose wages never caught up with prices.

Law's "success" with the Mississippi System was viewed with envy and fear from across the Channel in England. Britain, like France, had heavily encumbered itself, with the help of the Bank of England and Lottery loans, to fight the War of the Spanish Succession. The Bank of England was an innovator in the creation of paper money and checking accounts. Its entire capital base was made up of government debt, with its charter allowing it to issue notes up to the amount of its capital.

The Bank of England was constantly hounded by competitors who wanted a share of the Bank's lucrative business. One of these competitors was the Sword Blade Company, which was headed by Sir John Blunt. This Sword Blade Company was to serve as the credit creating arm of Blunt's South Sea Company. In 1711, this company was given the monopoly rights to trade with South America. Unfortunately, the Spanish were to greatly hinder the exploitation of this monopoly. In exchange for this monopoly, the company refinanced £9 million in government debt.

But this was just the beginning. In 1719, with total government debt well over £40 million, the South Sea Company proposed a massive refinancing of the government's debt, *à la* John Law. The Company was forced to bid against the Bank of England for this operation, and finally won out by offering extraordinary terms and extensive bribery. Once the bid had been won, the price of South Sea stock took off, which was necessary for Blunt's plan to work. The Company would make its money on the conversion, by exploiting the exchange difference between the government debt and inflated share prices.

The South Sea shares moved quickly to £1,000, with the aid of Company loans totaling £11 million, the government loaning £1 million, the Bank of England loaning money on its own stock and the Royal African company lending in £102,000. With plenty of money in Exchange Alley, there were plenty of promoters hawking what came to be known as "bubble companies." Eighty-eight of these companies were promoted just in the month of June, 1720.

The British government, at the urging of the South Sea Company, passed the Bubble Act which effectively shut down these upstart bubble companies. Ironically, the enforcement of this Act against four companies served to burst the bubble, and speculators rushed to sell. By December of 1720, South Sea stock was trading at £120.

The Company was bankrupt, and had no real quality assets to begin with, but speculators were not cognizant of this as the market began to feed on itself. This episode was, in relation to the Mississippi Bubble, short-lived. The difference being that the Bank of England, in an effort to raise needed liquidity, began calling in loans, not to mention not making new ones, and also offering interest-bearing notes to depositors, the equivalent of selling certificates of deposit in modern banking. John Law, with his Royal Bank, had taken the opposite strategy, by creating money to support the shares, which only prolonged the Mississippi Bubble crisis.

The explanation for the cause of speculative bubbles comes to us by examining the Austrian School's theory of the trade cycle. This theory, formulated by second generation Austrian economists, Ludwig von Mises and Friedrich A. Hayek, in fact has its roots, according to Mises, with the English "Currency School."[3] Unfortunately,

---

[3] Ludwig von Mises, "The Austrian Theory of the Trade Cycle," in *The Austrian Theory of the Trade Cycle and Other Essays*, David O'Mahony and J. Huston McCulloch, trans. (Auburn, Ala.: Ludwig von Mises Institute, 1983), p. 1.

the Currency School did not realize that unbacked bank accounts were equivalent to unbacked banknotes in terms of expanding excessive credit. Thus, as the Bank of England was forced to suspend payment on numerous occasions, it appeared that the Currency School's explanation of the trade cycle was erroneous, and the view that the trade cycle had nothing to do with money or credit, but instead Keynes's "animal spirits" came to the fore.

The key point of the Austrian trade cycle theory is that an increase in the supply of money engenders an economic "boom" followed subsequently by the correction of that malinvestment, or "bust," which is characterized by less money or credit. The business cycle is initially generated by some sort of monetary intervention in the market, typically in the modern world by bank credit expansion to business. However, this monetary intervention could be in the form of the following, listed by Gottfried Haberler:

(a) An increase of gold and legal tender money.

(b) An increase of banknotes.

(c) An increase of bank deposits and bank credits.

(d) An increase in the circulation of checks, bills, and other means of payment which are regularly or occasionally substituted for ordinary money.

(e) An increase of the velocity of circulation of one or all these means of payments.[4]

People, as they earn money, spend some on consumption, keep some in cash balances, while the rest is saved or invested in capital or production. For most people, this means setting aside a portion of their income by buying stocks, bonds, or bank certificates of deposits or savings accounts. People determine the amount they wish to put in savings by their time preferences, i.e., the measure of their preference for present, as opposed to future, consumption. The less they prefer consumption in the present, the lower their

---

[4] Gottfried Haberler, "Money and the Business Cycle," in ibid., p. 9.

time preference. The collective time preferences for all savers determines the pure interest rate. Thus, the lower the time preference, the lower the pure rate of interest. This lower time-preference rate leads to greater proportions of investment to consumption, and therefore an extension of the production structure, serving to increase total capital. Conversely, higher time preferences do the opposite, with high interest rates, truncation of the production structure, and an abatement of capital. The final array of various market interest rates are composed of the pure interest rate plus purchasing power components and the range of entrepreneurial risk factors. But the key component of this equation is the pure interest rate.

When a monetary intervention, as discussed above, occurs, the effect is the same as if the collective time preferences of the public had fallen. The amount of money available for investment increases, and with this greater supply, interest rates fall. In turn, entrepreneurs respond to what they believe is an increase in savings, or a decrease in time preferences. These entrepreneurs then invest this capital in "higher orders" in the structure of production, which are further from the final consumer. Investment then shifts from consumer goods to capital goods industries. Prices and wages are bid up in these capital goods industries. But the money does not immediately go into production, as Mises writes:

> The moderated interest rate is intended to stimulate production and not to cause a stock market boom. However, stock prices increase first of all. At the outset, commodity prices are not caught up in the boom. There are stock exchange booms and stock exchange profits. Yet, the "producer" is dissatisfied. He envies the "speculator" his "easy profit." Those in power are not willing to accept this situation. They believe that production is being deprived of money which is flowing into the stock market. Besides, it is precisely in the stock market boom that the serious threat of a crisis lies hidden.[5]

---

[5]Ludwig von Mises, *On the Manipulation of Money and Credit*, Bettina Bien Greaves, trans. (Dobbs Ferry, N.Y.: Free Market Books, 1978), p. 161.

Increases in the Supply of Money, Speculative Bubbles, and the Austrian Malinvestment Theory

This shift to capital goods industries would be fine if people's time preferences had actually lessened. But this is not the case. As the newly created money quickly permeates from business borrowers to wages, rents, and interest, the recipients of these higher incomes will spend the money in the same proportions of consumption-investment as they did before. Thus, demand quickly turns from capital goods back to consumer goods. Unfortunately, capital goods producers now have an increased amount of goods for sale and no corresponding increase in demand from their entrepreneurial customers. This wasteful malinvestment is then liquidated, typically termed a crash, bust or crisis, which is the market's way of purging itself, the first step back to health. The ensuing recession or depression is the market's adjustment period from the malinvestments back to the normal efficient service of customer demands.

This process or cycle can occur in a relatively short period of time. However, the booms are sometimes prolonged by more doses of monetary intervention. The greater the monetary expansion, both in magnitude and length of time, the longer the boom will be sustained (as was the case with the Mississippi Bubble).

The recovery phase, or recession, will weed out inefficient and unprofitable businesses that were possibly engendered by, or propped up by the money-induced boom. The recovery is also characterized by an increase in the "natural" or pure rate of interest. In other words, time preferences increase, which leads to a fall in the prices of higher-order goods in relation to those of consumer goods. As Rothbard writes:

> Not only prices of particular machines must fall, but also the prices of whole aggregates of capital, e.g., stock market and real estate values. In fact, these values must fall more than the earnings from the assets, through reflecting the general rise in the rate of interest return.[6]

---

[6]Murray Rothbard, *America's Great Depression*, 4th ed. (New York: Richardson & Snyder, 1983), p. 21.

In the final analysis, monetary intervention cannot increase the supply of real goods, it merely diverts capital from avenues the market would dictate toward wasteful malinvestment. The boom created has no solid base, and thus, "it is *illusory* prosperity."[7]

The three episodes discussed are examples of malinvestment at, in retrospect, its most ludicrous. All were created by different examples of monetary intervention. The Tulipmania was engendered and fueled by a massive influx of specie into Amsterdam; see Haberler's "a" above. The Mississippi Bubble was driven by a blizzard of John Law's paper; see "b" and "d" above. The South Sea Bubble was formed by the modern banking tools of deposits and credits, along with increasing, as Murphy relates: "the velocity of circulation of money by lending money to potential purchasers of its stock;" see "c" and "e" above.[8]

All three objects of speculation were equally dubious in terms of their investment value. With all due respect to Mr. Garber, in no way can a cogent argument be made to support how the value of a tulip bulb could be greater than the land it is grown in. John Law's Mississippi Company had the appearance of a powerful company, but the majority of its assets were the debts of a bankrupt country. As Wagner aptly puts it, "Counterfeiting becomes a profitable activity, one that the state customarily tries to reserve for its own use."[9] This counterfeiting was Law's only asset, but as we learned from Mises, it cannot create real prosperity. The South Sea Company, similar to the Mississippi Company, was capitalized with government debt and was technically bankrupt.

The busts, in all three cases, served to liquidate the malinvestments, the break being sharper in the Tulipmania and South Sea cases. In both these cases, a sound money alternative was available

---

[7] Mises, *On the Manipulation of Money and Credit*, p. 183.

[8] Antoin Murphy, *Richard Cantillon: Entrepreneur and Economist* (Oxford: Clarendon Press, 1986), p. 73.

[9] Richard E. Wagner, "Boom and Bust: The Political Economy of Economic Disorder," *The Journal of Libertarian Studies* 4, no. 1 (Winter 1980): 13.

for capital to flee to. In the Mississippi Bubble case, the only alternative to Law's worthless stock was his worthless currency. The ensuing recessions were painful, although short, and in the case of France, engendered a healthy distrust of paper money which served that country well. In the case of England's handling of the South Sea episode, a mistake was made in not allowing the full brunt of the crisis to be played out. This is a mistake that has been and continues to be repeated constantly throughout history. In times of financial panic a "lifeboat operation" is employed. As Mises explains:

> If the crisis were ruthlessly permitted to run its course, bringing about the destruction of enterprises which were unable to meet their obligations, then all entrepreneurs—not only banks but also other businessmen—would exhibit more caution in granting and using credit in the future. Instead, public opinion approves of giving assistance in the crisis. Then, no sooner is the worst over, than the banks are spurred on to a new expansion of circulation credit.[10]

Robert Walpole was possibly the originator of the "lifeboat operation" in 1721, and his legacy continues to live on in a modern world where we have unbacked fiat currency and central banking expanding and contracting—mostly expanding—the supply of money at every political whim. Thus, we live from one speculative bubble, or economic boom, to the next resounding crash, only to reinflate the supply of money, serving to maintain a shaky scaffolding under inefficient enterprise and bloated governments, forestalling the inevitable, complete bust.

Modern history is riddled with the occurrence of speculative bubbles and their inevitable crashes: Britain's railroad mania, the 1929 and 1987 stock market booms and subsequent crashes in the United States, Japan's stock market and property booms in the late 1980s. The common factor to all has been a monetary intervention or tremendous increase in the supply of money, ultimately leading to these malinvestments. These bubbles also share the common trait

---

[10]Mises, *On the Manipulation of Money and Credit*, p. 142.

that the object or manifestation of the monetary intervention was a familiar investment instrument, i.e., stocks and/or real estate—nothing as obscure as tulips, until recently that is, when the boom in China's stamp market was recently revealed.[11] The genesis for this bubble? Money, of course: it is estimated that savings deposits in China have grown to one trillion yuan. This vast increase in the supply of money has forced interest rates on bank savings accounts down to less than 2 percent! Thus, speculators and others have turned to stamps, pushing the price of some stamps up 500 percent in a two-year period.

With no contraction of China's monetary policy, the only thing that has stopped China's only free market is government coercion. The Chinese authorities began a crackdown to attempt to close down the market on November 9, 1991. Now Beijing's Yuetan Park is quiet, after being a site of trading activity as frenzied as that of the taverns of seventeenth-century Amsterdam, of Paris's Rue Quincampoix, or of London's Exchange Alley. But too much money must go somewhere, and China's stamp speculators are now trying to guess what the object of China's next bubble will be: stocks[12] or antiques.

As long as we live in a world in which the supply of money is being manipulated by governments, rather than set by the free and unfettered market, monetary interventions will continue to be the norm. Although much time has passed since the occurrence of the three episodes discussed in this paper, the laws of economics do not change with time. The consequences of monetary interventions have always been and will continue to be booms and subsequent busts. Speculative bubbles are the ultimate manifestation of these monetary induced booms. It is impossible to know what the object of the next speculative bubble will be, or exactly when it will occur.

---

[11]See James McGregor, "China Cancels Its Red-Hot Stamp Market, But Traders Hope Crackdown Will Pass," *Wall Street Journal* (December 19, 1991), p. C1.

[12]China has two stock exchanges, one in Shanghai, the other in Shenzhen; ibid.

What has been shown here is that these bubbles, or malinvestments, are engendered by increases in the supply of money, with the ensuing busts inevitably to follow, leading once again to bankruptcies and financial pain, as these wasteful investments are converted to more productive assets. What can be predicted with absolute accuracy is that fiat money, fractional-reserve banking, central banks, Keynesian monetary policies, and self-serving politicians will combine to ensure that there will be many more booms and speculative bubbles for future economists and historians to chronicle.

Bibliography

Andréadès, Andreas M. [1909] 1966. *History of the Bank of England 1640–1903*. New York: Augustus M. Kelley.

Bank of International Settlements. 1963. *Eight European Central Banks*. New York: Frederick A. Praeger.

Barbour, Violet. 1963. *Capitalism in Amsterdam in the 17th Century*. Ann Arbor: University of Michigan Press.

Bisschop, W.R. [1896] 1968. *The Rise of the London Money Market 1640–1826*. New York: Augustus M. Kelley.

Bloom, Herbert I. 1969. *The Economic Activities of the Jews of Amsterdam in the Seventeenth and Eighteenth Centuries*. New York and London: Kennikat Press.

Brewer, John. 1989. *The Sinews of Power: War, Money, and the English State, 1688–1783*. New York: Knopf.

Burke, Peter. 1974. *Venice and Amsterdam: A Study of Seventeenth-Century Elites*. London: Temple-Smith.

Calvo, Guillermo A. 1987. "Tulipmania." In *The New Palgrave: A Dictionary of Economics*. 4 Vols. Eds. John Eatwell, Murray Milgate, and Peter Newman. New York: The Stockton Press.

Carswell, John. 1960. *The South Sea Bubble*. London: The Cresset Press.

Clapham, Sir John. 1966. *The Bank of England: A History*. Volume I: *1694–1797*. London: Cambridge University Press.

Clough, Shepard B. 1968. *European Economic History: The Economic Development of Western Civilization*. New York: McGraw-Hill.

Clough, Shepard Bancroft, and Charles Woolsey Cole. 1952. *Economic History of Europe*. Boston: D.C. Heath.

Conant, Charles Arthur. [1927] 1969. *History of Modern Banks of Issue*. New York: Augustus M. Kelley.

Davis, Andrew McFarland. 1887. "An Historical Study of Law's System" I & II. *Quarterly Journal of Economics* 1 (April, July).

Davis, Ralph. 1973. *The Rise of the Atlantic Economies*. Ithaca, N.Y.: Cornell University Press.

Del Mar, Alexander. [1895] 1969. *History of Monetary Systems: A Record of Actual Experiments in Money Made By Various States of the Ancient and Modern World, as Drawn From Their Statutes, Customs, Treaties, Mining Regulations, Jurisprudence, History, Archeology, Coins Nummulary Systems, and Other Sources of Information*. New York: Augustus M. Kelley.

———. [1902] 1969. *A History of the Precious Metals, from the Earliest Times to the Present*. New York: Augustus M. Kelley.

De Vries, Jan. 1976. *Economy of Europe in an Age of Crisis, 1600–1750*. Cambridge: Cambridge University Press.

Dickson, P.G.M. 1967. *The Financial Revolution in England: A Study in the Development of Public Credit 1688–1756*. New York: St. Martin's Press.

Fisher, Kenneth L. 1987. *The Wall Street Waltz*. Chicago: Contemporary Books.

Flood, Robert P., and Robert J. Hodrick. 1990. "On Testing for Speculative Bubbles." *Journal of Economic Perspectives* 4, no. 2 (Spring).

Flynn, Dennis O. 1983. "Sixteenth-Century Inflation from a Production Point of View." In *Inflation Through The Ages: Economic, Social, Psychological and Historical Aspects*. Eds. Nathan Schmukler and Edward Marcus. New York: Brooklyn College Press.

Galbraith, John Kenneth. 1975. *Money: Whence It Came, Where It Went*. Boston: Houghton Mifflin.

Garber, Peter M. 1989. "Tulipmania." *Journal of Political Economy* 97, no. 3.

——. 1990. "Famous First Bubbles." *Journal of Economic Perspectives* 4, no. 2 (Spring).

Giuseppi, John. 1966. *The Bank of England: A History from its Foundation in 1694*. Chicago: Henry Regnery.

Groseclose, Elgin. 1961. *Money and Man: A Survey of Monetary Experience*. New York: Fredrick Unger.

Haberler, Gottfried. 1983. "Money and the Business Cycle." *The Austrian Theory of the Trade Cycle and Other Essays*. Auburn, Ala.: Ludwig von Mises Institute.

Hamilton, Earl J. 1929. "Imports of American Gold and Silver into Spain, 1503–1660." *Quarterly Journal of Economics* 43.

——. 1936. "Prices And Wages At Paris Under John Law's System." *Quarterly Journal of Economics* 51 (November).

——. 1937. "Prices And Wages In Southern France Under John Law's System." *Economic History Supplement to the Economic Journal* 3, no. 12 (February).

——. 1968. "Law, John." *International Encyclopedia of the Social Sciences*. Ed. David L. Sills. New York: Macmillan and The Free Press.

——. 1969. "The Political Economy of France at the Time of John Law." *History of Political Economy* 1.

Haring, Clarence H. 1915. "American Gold And Silver Production in the First Half Of The Sixteenth Century." *Quarterly Journal of Economics* 29 (May).

Hayek, F.A. 2008. *A Free-Market Monetary System and The Pretense of Knowledge*. Auburn, Ala.: Ludwig von Mises Institute.

Hayes, Carlton J.H. 1953. *Modern Europe to 1870*. New York: MacMillan.

Helfferich, Karl. [1927] 1969. *Money*. Trans. by Louis Infield. New York: Augustus M. Kelley.

Hildreth, Richard. [1837] 1968. *The History of Banks: To Which is Added, A Demonstration of the Advantages and Necessity of Free Competition in the Business of Banking*. New York: Augustus M. Kelley.

Horsefield, Keith J. 1982. "The 'Stop of the Exchequer' Revisited." *The Economic History Review* 15, no. 4 (November).

Hume, David. 1970. *Writings on Economics*. Ed. Eugene Rotwein. 2nd ed. Madison: The University of Wisconsin Press.

Keynes, John Maynard. 1964. *The General Theory of Employment, Interest, and Money*. New York: Harcourt, Brace & World.

Kindleberger, Charles P. [1978] 1989. *Manias, Panics, and Crashes: A History of Financial Crises*. New York: Basic Books.

———. 1984. *A Financial History of Western Europe*. London: George Allen & Unwin.

———. 1987. "Bubbles." In *The New Palgrave: A Dictionary of Economics*. 4 Vols. Eds. John Eatwell, Murray Milgate and Peter Newman. New York: The Stockton Press.

———. 1991. "The Economic Crisis of 1619 to 1623." *The Journal of Economic History* 51, no. 1 (March).

Law, John. [1705] 1966. *Money And Trade Considered with a Proposal for Supplying the Nation With Money*. New York: Augustus Kelley.

Mackay, Charles. [1841] 1932. *Memoirs of Extraordinary Popular Delusions and the Madness of Crowds*. London: Richard Bentley, New Burlington Street.

McCulloch, John C., ed. [1856] 1966. "Advice of His Majesty's Council of Trade, Concerning The Exportation of Gold and Silver in Foreign Coins & Bullion. Concluded 11th December, 1660." In *A Select Collection of Scarce and Valuable Tracts on Money*. New York: Augustus M. Kelley.

McGregor, James. 1991. "China Cancels Its Red-Hot Stamp Market, But Traders Hope Crackdown Will Pass." *Wall Street Journal*. December 19, 1991.

Melville, Lewis. [1921] 1968. *The South Sea Bubble*. New York: Burt Franklin.

Mises, Ludwig von. [1952] 1981. *The Theory of Money and Credit*. Trans. H.E. Batson. Indianapolis: LibertyClassics.

———. 1966. *Human Action: A Treatise on Economics*. 3rd ed. Chicago: Henry Regnery.

———. 1978. *On the Manipulation of Money and Credit*. Trans. Bettina Bien Greaves. New York: Free Market Books.

———. 1983. "The Austrian Theory of the Trade Cycle." *The Austrian Theory of the Trade Cycle and Other Essays*. Trans. David O'Mahony and J. Huston McCulloch. Auburn, Ala.: Ludwig von Mises Institute.

Mitchell, Wesley C. 1953. "The Role of Money in Economic History." In *Enterprise and Secular Change: Readings in Economic History*. Eds. Frederic C. Lane and Jelle C. Riemersma. Homewood, Ill.: Irwin.

Murphy, Antoin. 1986. *Richard Cantillon: Entrepreneur and Economist*. Oxford: Clarendon Press.

———. 1991. "The evolution of John Law's theories and policies 1707–1715." *European Economic Review* 34 (August).

Obstfeld, Maurice, and Kenneth Rogoff. 1983. "Speculative Hyperinflations in Maximizing Models: Can We Rule Them Out?" *Journal of Political Economy* 91, no. 4 (August).

Rich, E.E., and C.H. Wilson., eds. 1975. *The Cambridge Economic History of Europe*. Vol. 4: *The Economy of Expanding Europe in the Sixteenth and Seventeenth Centuries*. Cambridge: Cambridge University Press.

Richards, J.F., ed. 1983. *Precious Metals in the Later Medieval and Early Modern Worlds*. Durham, N.C.: Carolina Academic Press.

Rist, Charles. [1944] 1966. *History of Monetary and Credit Theory: From John Law to the Present Day*. New York: Augustus M. Kelley.

———. 1961. *The Triumph of Gold*. New York: Philosophical Library.

Rothbard, Murray N. 1983a. *America's Great Depression*. 4th ed. New York: Richardson and Snyder.

———. 1983b. "Economic Depressions: Their Cause and Cure." *The Austrian Theory of the Trade Cycle and Other Essays*. Auburn, Ala.: Ludwig von Mises Institute.

———. 1990. *What Has Government Done to Our Money?* 4th. ed. Auburn, Ala.: Ludwig von Mises Institute.

Salerno, Joseph T. 1991. "Two Traditions In Modern Monetary Theory: John Law And A.R.J. Turgot." *Journal des Economistes et des Etudes Humaines* 2 (June/September 1991).

Schama, Simon. 1987. *The Embarrassment of Riches*. New York: Alfred A. Knopf.

Schwartz, Anna J. 1973. "Secular Price Change in Historical Perspective." *Journal of Money, Credit, and Banking* 5, no. 1, part II (February).

Schubert, Eric S. 1988. "Innovations, Debts, and Bubbles: International Integration of Financial Markets in Western Europe, 1688–1720. *The Journal of Economic History* 48, no. 2 (June).

Smith, Adam. [1776] 1965. *An Inquiry into the Nature and Causes of the Wealth of Nations*. New York: Random House.

Smith, Vera C. [1936] 1990. *The Rationale of Central Banking and the Free Banking Alternative*. Preface by Leland B. Yeager. Indianapolis: Liberty Press.

Spooner, Frank C. 1972. *The International Economy and Monetary Movements in France, 1493–1725*. Harvard Economic Studies. Vol. 138. Cambridge, Mass.: Harvard University Press.

Van Cauwenberghe, E.H.G. 1983. "Inflation in the Southern Low Countries, from the Fourteenth to the Seventeenth Century: A Record of Some Significant Periods of High Prices." In *Inflation Through the Ages: Economic, Social, Psychological and Historical Aspects*. Eds. Nathan Schmukler and Edward Marcus. New York: Brooklyn College Press.

Van Horne, James C. 1985. "Of Financial Innovations and Excesses." *The Journal of Finance* 40, no. 3 (July).

Van Houtte, Jan A., and Leon Van Buyten. 1977. "The Low Countries." In *An Introduction to the Sources of European Economic History 1500–1800*. Eds. Charles Wilson and Geoffrey Parker. Ithaca, N.Y.: Cornell University Press.

Wagner, Richard E. 1980. "Boom and Bust: The Political Economy of Economic Disorder." *Journal of Libertarian Studies* 4, no. 1 (Winter).

Walker, Francis Amasa. [1886] 1968. *Money*. New York: Augustus M. Kelley.

Index

Aislabie, John, 94
amalgamation process, 26
Americas
    free coinage and, 21, 26–28, 107–08
    Mississippi Bubble and, 35, 56–57, 108
    South Sea Bubble and, ix, 88–89, 94, 109–10
America's Great Depression (Rothbard), 7n11, 113
Amsterdam, Bank of. *See* Bank of Amsterdam
"An Historical Study of Law's System" (Davis), 57n13, 62–63nn19–21, 4–65nn24–26
Andréadès, Andreas M., 81–83, 87, 102
    History of the Bank of England 1640–1903, 76–77nn2–5, 83–84nn21–23
Anne (Queen of England), 85
Astell, William, 100
Austrian School of economics, viii, 6, 110
Austrian theory of malinvestment, 9, 105–17
"The Austrian Theory of the Trade Cycle" (Mises), 110n3

Austrian theory of trade cycle, 6–8, 110–17

Bank of Amsterdam
    deposits into, 30f.
    effect on English economics, 75
    free coinage and, 22–33
    influence on John Law, 41–42, 107–08
Bank of England
    formation of, 77–79
    influence on John Law, 44–45, 47–49, 55, 74
    South Sea Bubble and, 79–03, 109–10
The Bank of England: A History (Clapham), 78n7–9
The Bank of England: A History from its Foundation in 1694 (Giuseppi), 77n6, 79–80nn13–15, 102n46
Bank of France. *See* Royal Bank (France)
bankruptcies in Holland, 32f.
Barbour, Violet, 27–29
    Capitalism in Amsterdam, 29n24
Blanc, Louis, 66–67

128 — *Early Speculative Bubbles and Increases in the Supply of Money*

Bloom, Herbert I., *The Economic Activities of the Jews of Amsterdam in the Seventeenth and Eighteenth Centuries*, 22n8
Blunt, John, ix, 86–88, 92–98, 109–10. *See also* South Sea Company
"Boom and Bust: The Political Economy of Economic Disorder" (Wagner), 114n9
Briscoe, John, 82
Brodrick, Thomas, 94
Bubble Act, ix, 100, 110
"Bubbles," *The New Palgrave: A Dictionary of Economics* (Kindleberger), 2n1
bullion. *See* precious metals
business cycle theory, 6–8, 110–17

Calvo, Guillermo, 11
The Cambridge Economic History of Europe, 20n1
Capitalism in Amsterdam (Barbour), 29n24
Carswell, John, 86–87, 92–94, 96–97
  The South Sea Bubble, 83n20, 101n43
Caswell, George, 88
central banks, vii
Chamber of Justice, 54–55
Chamberlain, Hugh, 82
Charles II (King of England), 76–77
Charles V (King of France), 19–20
"China Cancels Its Red-Hot Stamp Market, But Traders Hope Crackdown Will Pass" (McGregor), 116n11
China's monetary policies, 116

Clapham, John, 78–80
clipping of coins, 19, 80–81
Clough, Shepard B., 101, *European Economic History: The Economic Development of Western Civilization*, 22n11
coinage and recoinage, 8, 19–33, 39, 51, 80–83, 107–08
coins, gold and silver. *See* precious metals
Company of East Indies, 58
Company of the Indies. *See* Mississippi Company
Company of the West, 56–58, 108
Crowldy, Ambrose, 88
Currency School, 110–11

d'Arminy, Le Gendre, 56–58
Davis, Andrew McFarland, 64–66
  "An Historical Study of Law's System," 57n13, 62–63nn19–21
debasement of money, 19–20, 80–81
Del Mar, Alexander, 20, 26–27, 31, 107
  History of Monetary Systems, 21nn5–6
  A History of the Precious Metals, 29n25, 31nn26–27
Desmaretz, Nicolas, 39–40, 52–53
Dickson, G.G.M., 85–86, 98
  The Financial Revolution in England: A Study in the Development of Public Credit, 89–90nn33–34, 100nn41–42
Dillen, J.G. van, 30
Duke of Noailles, 53–55, 57

Duke of Orléans, 38, 39, 53
Dutch East India Company, 26–27

East India Company (English), 38, 44–45, 49, 85–87, 102
econometrics, 4, 105
The Economic Activities of the Jews of Amsterdam in the Seventeenth and Eighteenth Centuries (Bloom), 22n8
The Embarrassment of Riches (Schama), 32n28
English Copper Company, 100
European Economic History: The Economic Development of Western Civilization (Clough), 22n11, 101n44
Euvres complétes (Law), 73n38
"The Evolution of John Law's Theories and Policies 1707–1715" (Murphy), 45–46nn8–11
Exchange Alley, 99, 100, 110, 116

"Famous First Bubbles" (Garber), 4n6
Federal Reserve, vii
A Financial History of Western Europe (Kindleberger), 16–17
The Financial Revolution in England: A Study in the Development of Public Credit (Dickson), 85–86n24–27, 89–90nn33–34, 98n39, 100nn41–42
Flood, Robert, 4
Flynn, Dennis O., 27
free coinage, 8, 19–33. *See also* coinage and recoinage

A Free-Market Monetary System and The Pretense of Knowledge (Hayek), 8n14
Further considerations concerning raising the value of money (Locke), 82n17

Garber, Peter, 3–4, 11–15, 114
"Famous First Bubbles," 4n6
General Bank (of France), 51, 55–56, 108. *See also* Royal Bank (France)
The General Theory of Employment, Interest and Money (Keynes), 2–3, 106n1
Giuseppi, John, 77, *The Bank of England: A History from its Foundation in 1694*, 77n6, 79–80nn13–15, 102n46
Godfrey, Michael, 77
Godolphin, Sidney, 85–86, 88
gold. *See* precious metals
goldsmiths, 36, 63, 76–77, 80–83
Greenspan, Alan, 73
Gresham's Law, 20

Haberler, Gottfried, 111, 114
Hamilton, Earl J., 38n6
American Treasure and the Price Revolution in Spain, 28
"Imports of American gold and Silver into Spain, 1503–1660," 26n19
"Law, John," *International Encyclopedia of the Social Sciences*, 35n1, 39nn7–8
"The Political Economy of France at the Time of John Law," 52nn2–3, 57n12

"The Political Economy of France at the Time of John Law" (Hamilton), 58n14
"Prices and Wages At Paris Under John Law's System," 53n4, 70–71nn32–33, 72–73nn34–37
Harley, Robert, 86, 88–89
Hayek, Friedrich A., viii, 110
  A Free-Market Monetary System and The Pretense of Knowledge, 8n14
Helfferich, Karl, 20
Hildreth, Richard, *The History of Banks: To Which is Added, A Demonstration of the Advantages and Necessity of Free Competition in the Business of Banking*, 22n10
History of Modern Banks of Issue (Conant), 26n18
History of Monetary and Credit Theory: From John Law to the Present Day (Rist), 74n40
History of Monetary Systems: A Record of Actual Experiments in Money Made By Various States of the Ancient and Modern World (Del Mar), 20n2–3, 21nn5–6, 107n2
History of the Bank of England 1640–1903 (Andréadès), 76–77nn2–5, 81n16, 82–83nn17–19, 83–84nn21–23, 87n30
A History of the Precious Metals (Del Mar), 29n25, 31nn26–27
Hodrick, Robert, 4
Horsefield, Keith, 76–77
Huancavelica mercury mine, 26

Hume, David, 7, 27

"Imports of American gold and Silver into Spain, 1503–1660" (Hamilton), 26n19
inflation
  free coinage and, 27
  Mississippi Bubble and, 8, 46, 73–74, 96, 108–09
  severe weather and, 86
Inflation Through The Ages: Economic, Social, Psychological and Historical Aspects, 27n21
An Inquiry into the Nature and Causes of the Wealth of Nations (Smith), 22–25
The International Economy and Monetary Movements in France (van Dillen), 30
International Encyclopedia of the Social Sciences, 35n1

Keynes, John Maynard, 105–06
  The General Theory of Employment, Interest and Money, 2–3
Keynesian economics, 36, 69, 73, 105–06, 111, 117
Kindleberger, Charles, 1–2
  "Bubbles," *The New Palgrave: A Dictionary of Economics*, 2n1
  A Financial History of Western Europe, 16–17
  Manias, Panics, and Crashes: A History of Financial Crises, 15–16

land (as money), 42–44, 46, 80–83, 87

Land Bank project, 80–83
Law, John
    Bank of Amsterdam as inspiration, 33
    banking proposal, 38–40
    biographical information, 35–38
    effect on English economics, 87–88, 92, 96, 107–10
    Euvres complétes, 73n38
    Mississippi Bubble and, 3–4, 8, 51–74, 114–15
    monetary theories, 41–50
    overview, ix
"Law, John," (Hamilton), 35n1
Law, John, publications by
    Money and Trade Considered: With a Proposal for Supplying the Nation With Money, 38, 41–43
    The Present State of the French Finances, 68–69nn30–31
    Proposals and Reasons for constituting a Council of Trade, 37
    Theory of Money, 87–88
    "Treatise on Money and Commerce," 39
Le Gendre d'Arminy, 56–58
Locke, John, 82
London Exchange Alley, 99, 100, 110, 116
Louis XIV (King of France), 38–39, 51, 53, 85
Louisiana, 56–57, 108
"The Low Countries," *An Introduction to the Sources of European Economic History 1500-1800* (van Houtte and van Buyten), 33n29
Lowndes, William, 81–82

Mackay, Charles, ix, 11
    Memoirs of Extraordinary Popular Delusions and the Madness of Crowds, ixn1, 11, 36n2, 37n4, 38n6, 39nn7–8
Macleod, H.D., 87–88
    malinvestment, theory of, 9, 105–17
Malt Lottery, 84
Manias, Panics, and Crashes: A History of Financial Crises (Kindleberger), 15–16
Mary (Queen of England), 79
McCulloch, John C., *Principles of Political Economy*, 82n17
McGregor, James, "China Cancels Its Red-Hot Stamp Market, But Traders Hope Crackdown Will Pass," 116n11
Memoirs of Extraordinary Popular Delusions and the Madness of Crowds (Mackay), ixn1, 11, 36n2, 37n4, 38n6, 39nn7–8
Mexico, 26
Million Bank, 99
Mises, Ludwig von, viii, 6, 110, 112, 115
    On the Manipulation of Money and Credit, 114n7
Mississippi Company, ix, 48–50, 58–74, 108–110. *See also* Law, John
Money (Walker), 27nn22–23
money, defined, 7
"Money and the Business Cycle, 111
Money and Trade Considered: With a Proposal for Supplying the Nation With Money (Law), 39, 41–44

Montague, Charles, 77, 78
Murphy, Antoin, 5–6, 44–48, 54, 58–59, 66–68
  Richard Cantillon: Entrepreneur and Economist, 56–57nn10–11, 59–60nn15–16, 64nn22–23, 65n27, 73n39, 114n8

The New Palgrave Dictionary of Economics, 11
Noailles, Duke of, 53–55, 57
Norman, Montagu, 73

"On Testing for Speculative Bubbles" (Flood and Hodrick), 4nn7–9
On the Manipulation of Money and Credit (Mises), 112n5, 114n7, 115
Orléans, Duke of, 38, 39, 53

Paterson, William, 77–78
Philip, Duke of Orléans, 38, 39, 53
"The Political Economy of France at the Time of John Law" (Hamilton), 52nn2–3, 57n12, 58n14
Posthumus, N.W., 13–14
precious metals. *See also* coinage and recoinage
  compared to paper money, 48, 73–74, 82–83, 108
  free coinage, 19–33
  influx into Europe, 26–31
  monopoly by government bank, 61–65, 68, 80–83
  ties to U.S. dollar, vii

prices, 70–74
"Prices and Wages At Paris Under John Law's System" (Hamilton), 53n4, 70–71nn32–33, 72–73nn34–37
Principles of Political Economy (McCulloch), 82n17
Proposals and Reasons for constituting a Council of Trade (Law), 37

Rational Expectations School, 1–2, 4, 11, 105–06
Recoinage Act of 1696, 80–81
recoinage and coinage, 8, 19–33, 39, 51, 80–83, 107–08
Richard Cantillon: Entrepreneur and Economist (Murphy), 6n10, 54–55nn6–7, 56–57nn10–11, 64nn22–23, 65n27, 73n39, 114n8
Rist, Charles, 3
  History of Monetary and Credit Theory: From John Law to the Present Day, 74n40
Rothbard, Murray, viii, 7, 43
  America's Great Depression, 7n11, 113
  What Has Government Done to Our Money?, 7n13
Royal African Company, 99, 110
Royal Bank (France), 35–40, 49, 59–74, 108. *See also* General Bank (of France)
Royal Lustering Company, 100

Salerno, Joseph T., 73–74
"Two Traditions in Modern Monetary Theory: John Law and A.R.J. Turgot," 3n5

Schama, Simon, 31–32
  The Embarrassment of Riches, 32n28
silver. *See* precious metals
"Sixteenth-Century Inflation from a Production Point of View" (Flynn), 27
slave trade, 89
Smith, Adam, *An Inquiry into the Nature and Causes of the Wealth of Nations*, 22–25
South America. *See* Americas
South Sea Act, 90–91
The South Sea Bubble (Carswell), 83n20, 86–87nn28–29, 87n31, 92n35, 94–95nn36–37, 101n43
South Sea Company
  conversion Acts and, 90–96
  establishment of, 88–90
  framework of, 49
  increase and fall of share prices, 96–103
  increase in money supply and, 89–103
  influence on John Law, 45
  overview, viii, 8
  trade cycle theory and, 109–11
Stop of the Exchequer, 76–77
"The 'Stop of the Exchequer' Revisited" (Horsefield), 76n3
Strong, Benjamin, 73
Sword Blade Company, 86–88, 92, 109

theory of malinvestment, 9, 105–17
Theory of Money (Law), 87–88
time preference, 7, 111–13

trade cycle theory, 6–8, 110–17
"Treatise on Money and Commerce" (Law), 39
Tulipmania
  background, 11–17
  increase in money supply and, 19–33, 114–16
  malinvestment theory and, 106–08
  overview, viii–ix, 8
"Tulipmania" *Journal of Political Economy* 97 (Garber), 11–15nn2–11
"Tulipmania" *The New Palgrave: A Dictionary of Economics* (Calvo), 11n1
Tunnage Bank, 78–79. *See also* Bank of England
"Two Traditions in Modern Monetary Theory: John Law and A.R.J. Turgot" (Salerno), 3n5

United States, 35. *See also* Americas

van Buyten, Leon, 32–33
van Dillen, J.G., 30
van Houtte, Jan A., 32–33

wages, 70–74
Wagner, Richard E., 114
Walker, Francis Amasa, 27n21
Walpole, Robert, 92, 101, 115
War of Spanish Succession, 51–52, 85, 90, 108
Wealth of Nations (Smith), 22–25
Welsh Copper Company, 100

What Has Government Done to Our Money? (Rothbard), 7n13
William of Orange (King of England), 75–76, 79, 85
Writings on Economics (Hume), 7n12

York Buildings Company, 100